MAXnotes®

Margaret Atwood's

The Handmaid's Tale

Text by
Malcolm Foster
Professor of Canadian Literature
Concordia University
Montréal, Canada

Illustrations by
Karen Pica

Research & Education Association
Visit our website at
www.rea.com

Research & Education Association
61 Ethel Road West
Piscataway, New Jersey 08854
E-mail: info@rea.com

MAXnotes® for
THE HANDMAID'S TALE

Printed in the United States of America

Library of Congress Control Number 2006936791

International Standard Book Number 0-87891-232-0

What **MAXnotes** *Will Do for You*

This book is intended to help you absorb the essential contents and features of Margaret Atwood's *The Handmaid's Tale* and to help you gain a thorough understanding of the work. Our book has been designed to do this more quickly and effectively than any other study guide.

For best results, this **MAXnotes** book should be used as a companion to the actual work, not instead of it. The interaction between the two will greatly benefit you.

To help you in your studies, this book presents the most up-to-date interpretations of every section of the actual work, followed by questions and fully explained answers that will enable you to analyze the material critically. The questions also will help you to test your understanding of the work and will prepare you for discussions and exams.

Meaningful illustrations are included to further enhance your understanding and enjoyment of the literary work. The illustrations are designed to place you into the mood and spirit of the work's settings.

This **MAXnotes** book analyzes and summarizes each section as you go along, with discussions of the characters and explanations of the plot. A biography of the author and examination of the work's historical context will help you put this literary piece into the proper framework of what is taking place.

The use of this study guide will save you the hours of preparation time that would ordinarily be required to arrive at a complete grasp of this work of literature. You will be well prepared for classroom discussions, homework, and exams. The guidelines that are included for writing papers and reports on various topics will prepare you for any added work that may be assigned.

The **MAXnotes** will take your grades "to the max."

Larry B. Kling
Chief Editor

Contents

Each chapter includes List of Characters, Summary, Analysis, Study Questions and Answers, and Suggested Essay Topics.

MAXnotes® are simply the best – but don't just take our word for it...

"... I have told every bookstore in the area to carry your MAXnotes. They are the only notes I recommend to my students. There is no comparison between MAXnotes and all other notes ..."
 – *High School Teacher & Reading Specialist,*
 Arlington High School, Arlington, MA

"... I discovered the MAXnotes when a friend loaned me her copy of the MAXnotes for Romeo and Juliet. The book really helped me understand the story. Please send me a list of stores in my area that carry the MAXnotes. I would like to use more of them ..."
 – *Student, San Marino, CA*

"... The two MAXnotes titles that I have used have been very, very useful in helping me understand the subject matter reviewed. Thank you for creating the MAXnotes series ..."
 – *Student, Morrisville, PA*

A Glance at Some of the Characters

Offred

Commander's Wife
(alias Serena Joy)

Nick

Commander

Moira

Luke

Ofglen

Professor James
Darcy Pieixoto

SECTION ONE

Introduction

The Life and Work of Margaret Atwood

The 1960s opened the most dynamic period in Canadian writing, much as the 1920s did for American literature. One factor behind this upsurge was a sense that during World War II, 1939–1941, Canada had come of age and played a major role in defeating the Axis powers. Also, the Canada Council of the Arts, started at the end of the 1950s, provided grants that allowed young writers (many of whom grew up during the war) the time to research and write their books. Meanwhile, the explosion of post-war immigration, primarily from Europe, gave Canadian authors a much increased body of sophisticated readers.

Born in Ottawa, Canada's capital, in 1939, Margaret Atwood was part of this new wave of writers. She published her first book, *The Circle Game,* a collection of her poetry, in 1966, which won that year's Governor General's Award for poetry (these awards, affectionately called the GeeGees, are like the American Pulitzer Prize). The next year, Atwood was named writer-in-residence at Montréal's Sir George Williams University, the first of a series of such posts that allowed her to work almost full-time at her craft.

Because her father was an entomologist studying the insect life of Canada's forests, Atwood spent her childhood in a variety of places in northern Ontario and Québec before studying for her B.A. at the University of Toronto and her M.A. at Harvard's Radcliffe College. For the next few years, with her series of writer-in-residence posts, Atwood continued to live a semi-nomadic life. She seems to have thrived on it as a writer, publishing roughly a book a year since that time, although she and her partner, novelist

Graeme Gibson, and their daughter Jess have lived north of Toronto since the 1980s.

Atwood published her first novel, *The Edible Woman,* in 1969, and has become far more widely read as a novelist than as a poet. She continued to publish poetry, however, as well as two studies of Canadian writing, a book of history, and a number of children's books. In addition, she was one of the founders of the Writers Union of Canada, a lobby group, and served a term as its president.

Her childhood experience of northern Canada's long, harsh winters and enormous spaces, and her own rootlessness during those years, are themes that appear in virtually all of her novels and in much of her other writing. These themes are evident in her literary study, *Survival* (1972) and her poetry book *The Journals of Susanna Moodie* (1970). (Moodie, whose 1852 book *Roughing It in the Bush* is a Canadian classic of pioneer life in what was then a British colony, dwelt on the isolation and loneliness of settler life.)

Atwood's female protagonists, who frequently narrate their novels, live lonely and sometimes fearful lives in hostile environments, struggling to discover their identities and to assert themselves, with mixed results. They usually have to make some compromise with the world around them, rather than winning a clear victory, but they survive.

Most of Atwood's novels are set in the contemporary world. However, in *Alias Grace* (1996) her title character is a very young woman accused of aiding in the murder of her employer in mid-Nineteenth-Century Ontario. *Alias Grace* is based on an actual murder in 1843 and the subsequent trial. In *The Handmaid's Tale* (1985) Atwood projects a futuristic world of reaction and repression—and of virtual enslavement for women.

Historical Background

Nineteen hundred sixty-three was a revolutionary year for women around the world. The birth control pill became generally available, making it possible for women to lead active sex lives without a strong chance of pregnancy. That year, too, Betty Friedan published *The Feminine Mystique,* telling women, especially American women, that their lives were far more narrow and stifling than they should be. So the era of modern feminism began.

Of course, there had been many strongly independent women long before then. [They fought for decades for suffrage, a right most women in the U.S. and Canada weren't granted until the end of World War I (in Utah and Manitoba they won it much earlier)].

Friedan and the birth control pill revitalized the movement enormously, activating it in schools and universities, legislatures, businesses, and churches, with major success.

However, no revolutionary movement succeeds unopposed. The new feminism attracted many enemies, creating a reaction that was vocalized by women as well as men. Sometimes this reaction was couched in religious terms, in the idea that God had ordained men to be masters in the home and in religion—in fact, in every aspect of life. Some saw feminism as a threat to conventional morality and traditional family structure, and they were frightened and angry. Some men saw it as a threat to their own jobs.

Parallel in time to the rise of this new feminism was the development of television evangelism, usually of a very simplistic and conservative kind, with millions of believers sending in many millions of dollars to support "the good work." Probably the most popular of these was *The PTL Club* (Praise the Lord) hosted by Jim and Tammy Faye Bakker, until their involvement in financial and sexual scandals resulted in Jim's disgrace, trial, and imprisonment.

This American phenomenon of televised fundamentalist evangelism was matched by fundamentalist movements (some of which became increasingly militant and often violent) in several of the world's major religions including Hinduism, Islam, and various Christian denominations.

The most vivid example is the Islamic Revolution of 1979 in Iran, which brought to power the Ayatollah Ruhollah Khomeini and his crusade against Western "pollution" that included freeing women from their traditional role as wife, mother, and housekeeper. Many saw the new Islamic Republic of Iran as a reversion to the Middle Ages in its quest for a rigid, scripture-based society. Others saw it as a way of curbing the moral decay of a society that indulged itself with alcohol, drugs, and sexual promiscuity.

In the United States, religious fundamentalism became increasingly politicized, first in the "Moral Majority" and then in the "Christian Coalition," whose representatives strove to take control of local school boards, in particular. They also ran for public office, from small-town mayor to the U.S. Congress and Senate, with Reverend Pat Robertson vying for the Republican Party's presidential nomination in 1988. Millions saw this as the only way America could regain its sense of direction and its soul.

However, millions of others saw it as an assault on the U.S. Constitution itself, especially the constitutional principle of the separation of church and state and the tenet that there must be no established (i.e., dominant, state-supported) religion in the United States. This war of ideas continues today.

All these things went into Atwood's novel *The Handmaid's Tale*, her "what if" book. What if the religious right went beyond elections and staged a revolution, a *coup d'état*, and established an American government that replaced the Constitution with the Bible as its source of morality and law? What if it were as rigid and intolerant as Ayatollah Khomeini's regime in Iran? How could it take place? What would life be like under it, especially for women?

The Twentieth Century has had more than its share of brutal repression: Nazi Germany, Soviet Russia, Fascist Italy, etc. These dictatorships have used similar methods to control their people and destroy opposition. Atwood imagines her Republic of Gilead using many of these same methods, and even adding a few new ones of its own.

Atwood also looks at the increasing degradation of the world's environment: the pollution of its water, land, and air, which is having increasingly disastrous effects on human and animal life. Deserts are growing at a fearsome rate; rain forests are being demolished; greenhouse gases are causing global warming that results in melting glaciers, rising sea levels, climate changes, and the endangerment of species. Illegal or poorly managed toxic waste dumps are polluting groundwater, poisoning farm families' wells, and ruining land. Nuclear waste, with a killing life of hundreds or even thousands of years, is being produced each and every day, creating an increasingly threatening disposal problem. While Atwood's previous novels dealt with women searching for their identity, this book's protagonist has been stripped of hers. Her bank account has been frozen by the new state, and she loses her job since the new state forbids women to have a career. Her husband

and her young daughter have been taken from her. She is even dispossessed of her own name; instead, she had become merely Offred (of Fred, Fred's possession), named for the man to whom the government has temporarily assigned her, and she will be renamed for the next man to whom she is assigned. This is Gilead's reaction to feminism and to the problems that plagued U.S. society in the years prior to the revolution.

Master List of Characters

Offred—*narrator, former library-worker, separated by the authorities from her husband, Luke, and their five-year-old daughter; now Handmaid to the Commander.*

Luke—*Offred's husband, perhaps executed; Offred often thinks of him, remembering their past happiness as an escape.*

Their daughter—*unnamed; taken away from her parents and adopted by an establishment family.*

Offred's mother—*ardent feminist and single mother, rumored to have been exiled to Gilead's Colonies to die.*

Moira—*Offred's friend since college, a lesbian and ardent feminist, who escapes the Re-education Center (Red Center), but ends up as a state prostitute at Jezebel's.*

Commander—*formerly in marketing research, he helped create the Republic of Gilead and is one of its rulers, but is intrigued by Offred.*

Commander's wife (alias Serena Joy)—*once a soloist of a TV evangelism show, then a strident critic of American society; now arthritic and miserable, she is jealous of Offred.*

Nick—*Guardian and the Commander's chauffeur, he has a secret affair with Offred.*

Aunt Elizabeth and Aunt Sara—*guards at the Red Center.*

Aunt Lydia—*in charge of Handmaid-trainee indoctrination at the Red Center.*

Ofglen Number One—*Offred's grocery-shopping partner, who is involved in the underground Mayday organization and who tells Offred of its existence.*

Ofglen Number Two—*replacement for the first Ofglen; she keeps her distance from Offred.*

Ofwarren—*once named Janine, and a pet of the Aunts, she is the only Handmaid shown becoming a mother.*

Ofcharles—*a Handmaid who is hanged at a Salvaging ceremony for unknown crimes.*

Professor Maryann Crescent Moon—*the chair of the Twelfth Symposium on Gileadean Studies.*

Professor James Darcy Pieixoto—*the main speaker at the symposium.*

Summary of the Novel

A revolution has replaced the government of the United States with the Bible-based Republic of Gilead, a theocracy. The novel is narrated by a woman of 30 or so who has been separated from her husband and young daughter, then sent to a brainwashing center. She is trained to be a Handmaid, obliged to serve any member of the hierarchy as birth-mother of his children.

She is now on her third assignment, having failed to become pregnant in her previous two, so her time is running out. If she does not have a child soon, she will become an Unwoman, exiled to clean up toxic waste in one of the Colonies until she dies in two or three years. Unwomen, like Jews, African Americans, Catholics, and other groups considered undesirable by the Gilead regime are not allowed in Gilead.

As Offred, the narrator is a "walking womb" whose only duty is to help maintain the declining white population. She spends most of her time alone in her bare room remembering her previous life, and desperately seeking some means of escape from her new one, including suicide.

Although everyone in Gilead is a potential informer, Offred does establish a bond with another Handmaid, Ofglen, and with her master's chauffeur, Nick, with whom she has a secret affair. He arranges her escape via the Underground Femaleroad, which supposedly can help her get to freedom in Canada. In the last chapter two men come for her and take her from her master's house.

However, neither Offred nor the reader is sure if she is actually being rescued. Instead, she may be under arrest as an enemy of the state, and doomed to death.

This mystery is not cleared up in the "Historical Notes" that end the novel. These are concerned with a group of scholars in 2195 whose main interest is the study of Gilead as a historical phenomenon, not in the person Offred.

Estimated Reading Time

The Handmaid's Tale is divided into 46 short chapters plus a postscript. It is also divided into 15 numbered and named sections (e.g., "Shopping" and "Waiting Room"). Except for the postscript chapter, the novel is told in everyday speech, although the narrator does use a number of new terms invented by the new regime (e.g., "Unwoman" and "Prayvaganza"). The narrator also frequently uses irony and sarcasm, so sometimes she clearly means the opposite of what she says.

Parts I, II	1 hour
Parts III, IV	1 hour
Parts V, VI, VII	1 $^1/_2$ hours
Parts VIII, IX	1 $^1/_2$ hours
Parts X, XI	1 $^1/_2$ hours
Part XII	2 hours
Parts XIII, XIV, XV, Historical Notes	2 $^1/_2$ hours

The total reading time is approximately 11 hours.

SECTION TWO

Part I: Night

Chapter 1

New Characters:

Offred: *a newly assigned Handmaid, and the narrator*

Aunt Elizabeth and Aunt Sara: *guards at the Re-Education Center, armed with electric cattle prods*

Summary

It is night at the Rachel and Leah Re-education (Red) Center in the heartland of the Republic of Gilead. The Center, housed in a former high school, is where young white women are prepared for their role as replenishers of the population, Handmaids. On her army cot in the dormitory, once the school gym, Offred muses about what the room must have been like before Gilead.

She thinks about the basketball games played here, and how it must have looked decorated for school dances: the excitement, the fashionable clothing, the music. Now it's such a sad place, and so silent, since talking is forbidden.

As she often does, Offred remembers her past life, how as a teenager she yearned for the future with all its possibilities. Ruefully, she reminds herself that this Red Center, with its armed guards and barbed wire, is her future.

All she can yearn for now is an exchange of glances with the other inmates, even a few words with the armed Angels who stand

outside the fence with their backs firmly turned away from the exercise yard. But any Angel (Gilead's Gestapo) who looked at her or
spoke to her would be severely punished, as would she.

Instead, she thinks about the ways she and the other
Handmaids secretly communicate by furtive touch or silently
mouthing words, which the others lip-read. The one thing they
want to communicate is their real names, no longer allowed to
them. On her cot, Offred recites these names to herself.

Analysis

In this brief chapter, Atwood establishes the sense of fear and
repression in the new Republic of Gilead by emphasizing the differences between life in this society and life in earlier times. This
causes the reader to wonder how this situation came about.

The Red Center is like a reform school or prison, but with differences: in what prison are the guards called Aunts and prisoners
stripped of their names?

This raises the question: why must these women's names be
changed? What is going on here?

SECTION THREE

Part II: Shopping

Chapter 2

New Characters:

Rita: *a Martha (domestic servant) who resents Offred*

Cora: *also a Martha, but more sympathetic*

Commander's Wife: *the former TV singer Serena Joy, she is mentioned, but not yet seen*

Summary

Offred, recently arrived at her new posting, describes her room. Later it is indicated that this is her third posting to a Commander, and apparently each posting lasts somewhere between three and six months.

At this point, there is no clear indication as to how many postings a Handmaid has before it is concluded that she is infertile and ceases to be a Handmaid, but it is implied that when that happens she will be declared an Unwoman and exiled to one of Gilead's Colonies to clean up toxic waste and die.

In her room, Offred notes that there is nothing from which a rope can be hung; apparently Gilead authorities want to prevent any chance of a Handmaid's suicide. She also notes that there is no glass in front of the watercolor of blue irises, her window glass is shatterproof, and the windows can only be opened enough to let in air, but without room for escape. Although there are a few homey touches—the watercolor and a hooked rug on the floor—the room is just another prison cell, but better than a dormitory. At least she has privacy.

Here, as at the Red Center, time is measured for her by bells. When the bell rings, she dons her Handmaid uniform. It is an ankle-length red gown and a white, winged headdress that allows her only to see straight ahead and prevents others from seeing her. With these she wears red gloves and low-heeled red shoes. She thinks that this costume makes her look like a fairytale figure.

As she goes downstairs to the kitchen, she remarks that her door is unlocked and, in fact, won't close properly. In the kitchen, Rita is kneading dough, wearing the Martha uniform—a long green gown and white apron. Rita merely nods to Offred and hands her three shopping tokens for eggs, cheese, and meat.

In the kitchen, Offred must suffer Rita's surliness. Rita disapproves of Handmaids on moral grounds because they act as a sort of prostitute for the country. The Handmaids, however, have no other choice; if they refuse to be handmaids, they would be sent to certain death in the Colonies. Offred longs to help Rita knead the bread, but she knows Rita would be too afraid of the consequences to allow it.

Despite the abuse, Offred enjoys spending time in the kitchen with Rita and Cora. Offred fantasizes about drinking coffee, gossiping about neighbors, and discussing their aches and pains with Rita and Cora. Offred knows, however, that she cannot grow close to them as the Marthas are not allowed to fraternize with the Handmaids.

Analysis

This chapter makes clear that these young mothers (for Handmaids are recruited from women of proven fertility) had the choice of becoming Handmaids or Unwomen doomed to an agonizing death. It is clear that most, if not all, of the Handmaids are unhappy with this new life because all means of escape or suicide have been eliminated.

Offred's remark that Commanders' homes have real coffee shows that Gilead is having problems maintaining its former standard of life. Perhaps other countries, including the coffee-growing ones, are boycotting the new government. Or perhaps the resistance movements, that will be described later, have cut the trade routes or damaged shipping facilities.

Rita's coldness to Offred shows that it is not just Handmaids who are unhappy in Gilead. Offred's remark that Marthas cannot fraternize with Handmaids is the first of many signals that Gilead operates on the principle of divide and conquer.

Chapter 3

Summary

Offred goes on her shopping trip via the back door, past the garden where the Commander's arthritic Wife often works, although she leaves the hard digging to a Guardian. Guardians work as both police and as aides to Commanders. They are too young, too old, or too unfit for military service. The Wife's only other activity seems to be knitting scarves for Angels at the war front. Offred envies both of her pastimes.

She recalls first meeting the Wife when she was brought to the front door five weeks ago. This was the only time she was allowed to use the front door, and the Wife's hostility was immediately evident. The Wife warned Offred not to give her any trouble, dashing her hopes of viewing the Wife as an older sister or a motherly figure. Offred also noticed that the Wife was smoking, which is forbidden to Gilead's women.

Offred felt a sense of recognition, then suddenly realized that the Wife use to be the lead soprano on a Sunday morning TV show, called the *Growing Souls Gospel Hour*, and later became a scathing critic of the American way of life who foreshadowed the Gilead revolution. Her name was Serena Joy, Offred recalled. Serena Joy's fanaticism suggested to Offred that her new situation might be worse than her previous two.

Analysis

Although once a very active force in the anti-American

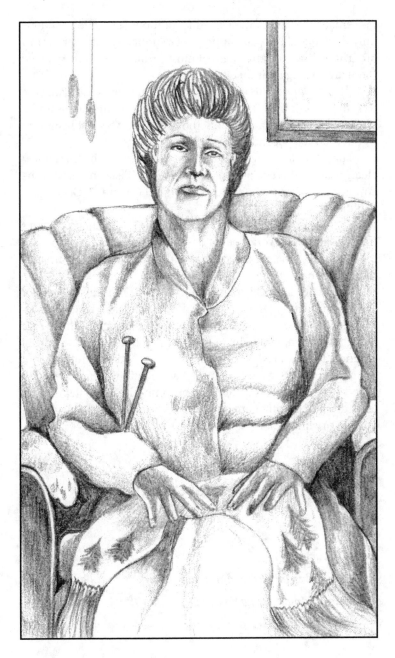

movement that led to the Gilead revolution, Serena Joy can now only garden and knit, and appears very unhappy with her narrow life. This echoes the aftermath of most revolutions: those who led them are among their first victims.

Having Handmaids (and probably Marthas and Guardians) use only the back door is like the situation of African Americans under slavery and after: refusing them the front door was a constant reminder of their second-class status.

That Serena Joy's scarves are sent to Angels "at the front lines" clearly shows there is armed resistance to Gilead in parts of the country, and echoes the coffee shortage of Chapter 2. Gilead is in trouble.

Serena Joy's hostility toward Offred, like Rita's, shows Gilead's fracture lines: everyone seems hostile toward, and suspicious of, everyone else. The regime's policy of divide and conquer appears to be working.

The Republic of Gilead is named after the biblical land east of the Jordan River, home of the children of Ishmael. Its grasslands made excellent pasture for cattle and sheep, and it was the source of spices, myrrh, and balm, a tree resin with medical use to heal wounds. In Joshua 22:38 it is referred to as "a city of refuge," but later, in Hosea 6:8, it has become a place of iniquity, "polluted with blood." So this promised land has become a hell. The Republic of Gilead, then, is aptly named: it has betrayed its promise and become a prison, even for its founders.

Chapter 4

New Characters:

Nick: *Guardian employed as the Commander's chauffeur*

Ofglen: *Handmaid assigned elsewhere and Offred's shopping companion*

Summary

Heading from the back door to the street, on her way to shop, Offred notices the Guardian Nick washing the Commander's car, a Whirlwind (like the other two cars available in Gilead, the Chariot and Behemoth, this model takes its name from the Bible). She thinks that Nick must have low status since he hasn't been issued an Econowife and lives alone in an apartment above the garage. She also notes an unlit cigarette in his mouth and guesses he, too, has something to sell on the black market.

She is startled when he winks at her and worries that he might be an Eye (Gilead's Gestapo-like secret state police) out to get her.

At the corner she waits for Handmaid Ofglen, recalling Aunt Lydia's words, "They also serve who only stand and wait." Then Ofglen joins her. Offred is wary of her, for she appears to be one of Gilead's true believers, so Offred speaks to her as little as possible. Ofglen remarks on the military campaign against Baptist rebels in the Blue Hills. Although afraid to talk, Offred is hungry for any news of the outside world, even if it may not be true.

On their way to the shop, they halt at one of the many armed barricades dotting the city streets, where Guardians inspect their passes in the Compuchek. Offred defies the rules slightly by meeting the eyes of one of the guards, and swaying her hips as she passes through the gate, for she enjoys the passive power she has over them. But she also wonders about these two very young Guardians, denied wives or any real contact with women, and can't help feeling pity for them.

Analysis

Offred's fear of Nick when he winks at her, and of Ofglen, is more evidence of the paranoia that permeates Gilead. How can people organize opposition to the regime if they can trust no one, if anyone may be an informer? And yet Ofglen's talk of the Baptist resistance shows that some people have managed to organize themselves against Gilead and have even armed themselves.

The barricade's Compuchek shows another means by which Gilead controls society. This Bible-based regime is quite ready to use modern technology to control its citizens. That Gilead still manages to make cars and uses technology for repression shows

that, even if there are shortages and rebellions, Gilead is by no means on the brink of industrial collapse.

Offred's ambiguous feelings toward the Guardians at the barricade show that, although she hates Gilead, she is also aware that those who enforce the rules are similarly locked into lives that are less than fulfilling.

Aunt Lydia lies when she implies that "They also serve who only stand and wait" is from the Bible. In fact, it was written by seventeenth-century poet John Milton, ironically an ardent defender of individual liberties. This is the first of several instances where Gilead has changed the Bible to suit its purposes. For a regime that claims the Bible as the foundation of its laws, to lie about the Bible and its contents shows that Gilead not only is brutal, but is totally corrupt as well. Gilead is built on lies.

Chapter 5

New Character:

Ofwarren: *(formerly Janine) Handmaid who was trained at the Red Center with Offred; she is now pregnant*

Summary

Offred and Ofglen's trip takes them through an upper-middle-class neighborhood, and Offred notices there are no children to be seen or heard. This once was a neighborhood of lawyers, doctors, and professors, but Offred notes that Gilead has no more lawyers, and the university is closed. She also notes that there are very few older women to be seen.

She reminds herself that the streets are safe for women, as they never were before. She remembers Aunt Lydia's statement that there are two kinds of freedom—freedom *from* and freedom *to*—and that the freedom women have in Gilead from the fear of rape and molestation should not be underrated.

They pass Lilies of the Field, a store whose sign has only a

picture of a lily, with the words painted out. All signs are like this: any writing has been obliterated because women are no longer permitted to read. Then they enter Milk and Honey, where she is surprised to find oranges—the war has made California oranges unobtainable and few shipments come from Florida due to sabotage of the railroads.

Among the various Handmaids in the store is a pregnant one, whom Ofglen identifies as Ofwarren. Offred recognizes her as Janine from the Red Center, who was one of Aunt Lydia's pets. Although the Handmaids pretend delight at Ofwarren's pregnancy, Offred sees they really are jealous of her and that Janine is gloating.

At All Flesh, Offred buys a stringy chicken, remarking that plastic bags are no longer used for wrapping groceries. This reminds her of the stacks of plastic bags she saved which her husband Luke feared their daughter might pull over her head.

On their way home, they encounter a Japanese trade delegation of men and women. The women's dresses—short skirts and high heels—overwhelm her. An interpreter asks if the two Handmaids will pose for photographs, but they refuse. Then the translator asks, for one of the Japanese, if the Handmaids are happy. "Yes," Offred replies, "we are very happy."

Analysis

The lack of children is a reminder of Gilead's population crisis. Although the decline of white births was a central reason for the revolution, Gilead hasn't been able to raise the birthrate.

The shortage of older women is more frightening perhaps. Since they are beyond childbearing age, Gilead has sent them to the Colonies to die. While Marthas are older women, Gilead only needs a certain number of household servants, so perhaps the surplus is eliminated.

Aunt Lydia's statement about two kinds of freedom raises an important point. Offred agrees that the streets are now safe for women; they are free from fear of molestation or attack. But they are not free to live their own lives, make their own decisions, or live where and as they choose. So her former freedom *to* has been replaced by freedom *from*, and it is clear which sort of freedom

Offred would choose if she could. She wants back her freedom to choose a life of her own making.

The disruption of trade due to war and sabotage shows the extent of opposition to the regime. All of Central America is at war with Gilead, and California is in rebel hands.

The presence of the Japanese trade delegates in Gilead suggests that the government is dependent on foreign trade. That the Japanese women can go out in public in their normal clothes must mean that Gilead needs trade more than it needs women to be politically correct by wearing ankle-length gowns. Although its universities, and probably its laboratories are closed, Gilead still needs high-tech devices to keep tabs on its citizens, and probably has to look to Japan for its equipment. Maybe even its Whirlwind cars are actually made in Japan.

Of all the Handmaids seen, Ofwarren is the only one who is pregnant. This suggests that the Handmaid idea isn't working, and the population slide is continuing.

The disappearance of lawyers, possibly by execution, means that the legal system is entirely in the hands of Gilead's hierarchy, with no possibility of legal appeal against its laws. The closing of the university and its conversion into barracks and concentration camp bodes ill for Gilead. Society needs trained, imaginative people to create the means by which it maintains and critiques itself. By closing the universities, Gilead is dooming itself to extinction. But imagination and inventiveness are what Gilead fears most of all, so it has no choice.

Chapter 6

Summary

After they shop, Ofglen tells Offred she would like to pass the old nearby church—she would like to take the long way home, past the Wall. On their right is the river, with boathouses from which students used to launch their racing sculls. They pass the former dormitories and the football stadium. Offred notes that the stadium is now used

for Men's Salvagings (she only tells later what these are).

They pause briefly before the church, which is now used as a museum. Beyond is the Wall, once the boundary of the university, but now rigged with barbed wire, floodlights, and sentries.

Several figures are hanging on the Wall, their heads shrouded in white sacks. Blood has seeped through the bag covering one person's head, giving it the look of a grotesque smile. The three wear lab coats and carry signs with pictures of fetuses on them; evidently they were abortionists, and Offred wonders who informed on them. Gilead calls such men "war criminals", even though their "crimes" were committed when abortion was legal. Offred is surprised that she feels nothing in their presence except fascination with that bloody grin. Ofglen's tremor surprises her; evidently she is moved by the sight of these executed men.

Offred remembers Aunt Lydia saying that they will get used to the new ways; in time, everything will become ordinary to them.

Analysis

Stringing up the bodies on the Wall of what was once a university seems to be Gilead's way of warning people not to break its laws, but is also a clear sign of how unpopular the new regime is. Only a vicious and frightened despot would do such a thing.

It also makes clear how completely opposite Gilead is to the biblical haven of Gilead where, in the words of the hymn, "all is peace." The only peace in Gilead is death.

A close look at the boathouses, the nearby church with its ancient burial ground, and the famous wall surrounding the university suggests that the university is Harvard. Harvard University, founded in 1636, was America's first, and one of the world's most famous institutions of higher learning. That Gilead has turned Harvard into a prison is obscene, and shows what Gilead is all about: repression, not enlightenment.

Ofglen's tremor at the sight of the dead is Offred's first clue that her shopping companion may not be a true believer.

Study Questions

1. Why does Offred want to recall the games and dances that were held in the former gymnasium that is now the Rachel and Leah Re-education (Red) Center?

2. Why are the Handmaid-trainees housed in the gym rather than the classrooms, and why are the cots in the Center set up with space between them?

3. Offred explores the room she has been assigned and discovers that the chandelier has been removed, the window glass is shatterproof, and the window only opens halfway. Why have these measures been taken?

4. What clothing is worn by the Handmaids and by the Marthas, and why are these outfits so important to the regime?

5. What does Offred remember of the Commander's Wife from the past, and why does Atwood choose to make this Wife a person who was famous in the time before the revolution?

6. Why does Serena Joy spend all of her time gardening and knitting scarves for the soldiers, and why is Offred envious of these pastimes?

7. Why does Offred fear that Nick is a spy? What would he be spying on?

8. Since Gilead is a fundamentalist Christian regime, why would the Baptists rebel against it?

9. Why are all the words banished from store signs? Why are Handmaids forbidden to read and write?

10. Why might Gilead have shipped most of its older women to the Colonies?

Answers

1. Offred recalls the games and dances to keep her memories of the past alive. Remembering serves as both an act of rebellion against Gilead and a way for her to maintain her sense of selfhood and sanity. She can easily recall the yearning teenager she once was, someone who looked forward to leaving home and starting her own independent life, because having been reduced by the Gilead regime to the status of a helpless child, she again yearns for independence.

2. The Handmaid-trainees are forbidden to talk with each

other; it is far easier to enforce this rule if they live in a single dormitory room. It would be impossible to monitor them with the same strictness if they were housed six or eight to a room. There are spaces between the cots to further ensure their silence and their obedience, but the women still manage to communicate by touching each other's hands across space, lipreading, and exchanging their names.

3. The alterations have been made to the room to keep a Handmaid from attempting an escape through suicide. That these precautions are automatically taken suggests the unhappy existence of the Handmaids since many of them must have resorted to this desperate measure.

4. The Handmaids are dressed in red, ankle-length dresses, red gloves, and red shoes. They wear white wings around their faces that limit their perspective and prevent them from being seen by others. The Marthas wear long, dull green dresses without the white wings; nobody cares if their faces are seen. Since the Handmaids and Marthas are servants of the state, their clothing must reflect their status. Most totalitarian societies put their people, even children, in uniforms to remind them of where their primary allegiance should be. This also serves to prompt children to inform on their parents, their siblings, and their friends, an important part of totalitarianism.

5. Offred recalls that the Commander's Wife was formerly Serena Joy—a television Gospel singer and later a critic of the American way of life. This realization suggests to Offred that her new situation might be worse than her previous two. That Serena Joy once had a career and fame makes her position as a Wife all the more ironic. Having railed against the values of American life, and promoted the values that Gilead goes on to adopt, she finds herself almost as much a prisoner of those values as any Handmaid is. Besides, just as with Serena Joy's husband, the Commander, Atwood wants to show how the initiators of Gilead are having to cope with the new regime. From top to bottom, Gilead is one giant prison.

6. Having led a very active life before the revolution, Serena Joy is reduced to just two things: gardening and knitting. By giving her arthritis as well, Atwood seems to be saying this once-powerful woman has stripped herself of all that power and now leads a pitifully narrow life. She knits useless scarves just to pass the time, in a small way killing the emptiness of her life. Offred envies these pastimes because they remind her of hobbies she had in the past and also because her present life is filled with meaningless waiting.

7. Nick's cockiness, his whistling, and the wink he gives Offred all add up to his being someone who doesn't fit what he is supposed to be. Since in Gilead everyone must fit in, Offred naturally thinks Nick is more than he appears, so he must be suspect. Gilead is full of informers; Handmaid-trainees are encouraged in this. Offred quite naturally would think he is spying on her, even though there is little reason for Gilead to assign a spy to her, simply because it teems with paranoia, as do all dictatorships.

8. While it is possible that conservative Baptists might have supported Gilead at the start, it is likely that they would have broken with the regime early on when they saw the way the Bible was being distorted and rewritten, and perhaps for other reasons as well. There is no worse enemy than one who has been betrayed, and Gilead is a betrayer of conservative Christianity. For the regime, religion is only a means to achieve power. The Bible is merely a weapon in their hands to keep people in line, and they feel free to adapt it to their needs, rather than adapt themselves to it.

9. Handmaid were similar to slaves in the antebellum South. Slave states in the antebellum South forbade the teaching of reading and writing to slaves. Thus, they had no access to subversive writings, such as those of Northern abolitionists, or to any books or journals dealing with freedom and human rights. They could only communicate with fellow slaves by word of mouth, which limited the chance of rebellion and made any concerted uprising impossible. Writing helps one to develop ideas as well as to communicate them. In Gilead,

women, and Handmaids especially, are not supposed to have ideas.

10. Gilead probably has a surplus male population that has to find employment. So it would also have a surplus female population, especially since women are not allowed to hold jobs. Because it regards women as second-class citizens, it can kill two birds with one stone by sending older women to the Colonies: it gets the toxic waste cleaned up and it has thousands fewer mouths to feed from a diminishing stock of food.

Suggested Essay Topics

1. Discuss why Atwood has set her novel in Cambridge, Massachusetts, home of Harvard University. What does this add to the novel?

2. Atwood chose not to follow a strictly chronological pattern in the telling of Offred's story. Why do you think she did so? What does it add and what are its disadvantages?

3. Aunt Lydia says to the Handmaid-trainees, "We were a society dying of too much choice." How does this relate to her distinction between freedom *from* and freedom *to*? What freedoms does Gilead claim to be providing its citizens? What freedoms are being denied?

Part III: Night

Chapter 7

New Characters:

Moira: *Offred's feminist friend from college*

Offred's mother: *single mother and ardent feminist*

Offred's unnamed daughter

Summary

Offred lies on her bed, feeling this time is her own; there are no signal bells, nothing to stop her reveries. She can let her thoughts drift back to the happier past.

She recalls working on a term paper, and Moira suggesting they go for a beer, which they do, with Offred's money.

Then she remembers a demonstration her mother took her to as a child. A crowd of mostly women was throwing magazines on a bonfire. A woman urged Offred to throw a magazine on the fire and she did. She glimpsed at some of the magazine's contents—pornography—but she was too young to know what it meant.

Her next recollection is much more painful: the time her daughter was taken from her. Offred appears to have been sedated and not really aware of what was happening. Although she was told her daughter would be well cared for, she believed the girl had been killed.

Returning to the present, she says she wishes this were only a made-up story she is telling. Then she would have some control over its events and outcome. She wonders if the story is truth or fiction. She knows it is both the truth and a story she is telling in her head. Telling a story implies an audience, she thinks. She thinks it would be comforting to imagine someone reading her story, thus forging a link with another person.

Analysis

Her memory of Moira is important to Offred, for it shows her experiencing the comradeship she now misses so desperately. And it shows she once had freedom to choose: to finish her term paper or go for a beer with Moira. Last, it shows she once could think and write and make her own future.

The memory of the pornography burning implies the idea of women as sexual prey, and shows people trying to reject these images.

Offred's memory of losing her daughter shows that Gilead managed the abduction by drugging her so that she couldn't resist. The statement that the child "will be in good hands" probably is true; she likely has been given to some childless Wife, one of the perks of rank.

Offred's confusion about the truth of her story shows the toll her life is taking on her. Inability to distinguish fact from fiction is generally a sign of mental illness. Perhaps Offred is close to losing her grip on reality.

Part IV: Waiting Room

Chapter 8

Summary

On another shopping trip, Ofglen and Offred again pass the Wall, which bears three new corpses, one in a Roman Catholic priest's black cassock. The other two bear purple placards that signify "Gender Treachery" (homosexuality), and are wearing Guardian uniforms.

Later Ofglen remarks, "It's a beautiful May day." While agreeing with Ofglen, Offred recalls that Mayday used to be a distress call. Luke once told her it came from the French phrase *M'aidez*, and this detail causes her to remember sharing coffee and the papers with him on lazy Sunday mornings.

They pass a funeral procession of Econowives, one bearing a black jar carrying a dead embryo from a stillbirth. Econowives, Offred reminds herself, dislike Handmaids.

Back home, Offred passes Nick, who is polishing the car. Nick asks her, "Nice walk?" and Offred nods. She says nothing since they are not allowed to talk to each other. She remembers Aunt Lydia's contemptuous remark about men and their sexuality: "They can't help it."

At the back of the house, Offred sees Serena Joy. She recalls how Serena Joy once made speeches about how women's proper place was in the home. Luke and Offred used to watch her on television, weeping, mascara running down her cheeks. Offred wonders if Serena Joy appreciates the irony that she was taken at her word and now is just another woman stuck at home.

She remembers one of Aunt Lydia's lessons: that Wives will resent Handmaids because Wives are unable to have children, but Handmaids can. Aunt Lydia urges the Handmaids to be patient and sympathetic if the Wives are unkind.

In the kitchen, Offred finds Rita peeling carrots, and she envies the sharp knife she uses, remarking to herself that this house is full of envy. Rita reminds her that this is bath day.

Upstairs in the hall, Offred is surprised to find a man standing there, his back turned. She recognizes him as the Commander, standing by her door, where he is not allowed to be. She wonders what he's doing there. Has he been in her room? What does this breaking of the rules mean?

Analysis

The three new corpses on the Wall show that Gilead's enemies include Roman Catholics and homosexuals, and the two dead Guardians show that even Gilead's own police cannot be trusted to obey its laws.

It is not surprising that Gilead hates homosexuality, since its principal aim is to breed new white babies. But it is surprising that it also targets Catholic priests. Clearly Gilead tolerates no deviation from its own state religion.

Ofglen's comment, "It's a beautiful May day," seems innocuous, for Offred has already remarked to herself what a nice day it is. It's surprising that Ofglen says it at all, though, since Handmaids are supposed to converse only when necessary. But Offred's linking that remark with the idea that Mayday is a distress signal will later prove to be significant.

The funeral of the Econowife's stillborn child is another reminder of the problems with fertility in Gilead. And Offred's comment that Econowives resent Handmaids refers to the divisions that permeate Gilead society.

Nick's "Nice walk?" verifies Offred's earlier feeling that he is not a typical Guardian. Is he dangerous, trying to provoke her into breaking the rules so he can report her, or is he a bit of a rebel? She will have to be very wary of him.

Offred's fascination with Rita's knife shows Offred's desperation. Perhaps she would use it to commit suicide; perhaps she would wield it to slash at her oppressors, the Commander and Serena Joy; perhaps she wants it as a means of escape to Canada. In any case, it would give her a sense of power and choice, the things that Gilead has done its best to strip from her.

The wordless encounter with the Commander outside her bedroom suggests that even Commanders are unhappy with the rules they themselves have put in place. But she doesn't know why he was there.

Chapter 9

Summary

Offred tells of her first exploration of her room after she moved in. It reminds her of motel rooms she and Luke shared before they were married. She remembers killing time waiting for Luke to arrive. She explores her room as slowly as possible, because it is the only excitement in her life.

In a corner of the closet floor some words are scratched: *Nolite te bastardes carborundorum*. Although she has no idea what this means, merely the fact that it is there is enough to excite her. It links her with the room's previous tenant, another Offred. Her predecessor had scratched those words to communicate with *her*, to establish a bond.

After finding this message, Offred muses on what this other Offred was like, and envisions her as vital as Moira. She even imagines her with freckles. Later she asks Rita about "the one with freckles." Rita replies, "She didn't work out," but will say nothing more. Still, Offred has the pleasure of knowing that her wild guess was right.

Analysis

Offred's slow, careful search of her room, spinning it out as long as possible, demonstrates just how empty and boring a Handmaid's life is. Finding that message is the first sign she has seen since her capture that someone cares about her, not just her reproductive capacity, and wanted to communicate with her so much that she went to considerable risk to scratch out this message.

Offred's depiction of her predecessor shows how much this link means to her: she has to give form and character to a woman whom she will never see and who, indeed, may even be dead. But any companionship is better than none.

Rita's curt response to Offred's question may be her ordinary manner with Handmaids, or may mean that what happened to the other Handmaid is too awful to talk about.

Chapter 10

Summary

Singing to herself, Offred remembers the first lines of the hymn "Amazing Grace," especially the fourth line, "Was bound, but now am free." She thinks about the word "free," and of other words now banned in Gilead. She also remembers an old song from a tape of her mother's with the line, "I feel so lonely I could die," which is precisely what she feels now: death is far more preferable to this emptiness and idleness. And she remarks that there isn't much music in this household.

It's a sunny, warm day in May, which makes her remember how she and her friends would peel down to tan as much of their bodies as possible, and how, later, Aunt Lydia said how awful it was that young women had once slathered themselves with oil, like basted meat.

This reminds her of college and Moira's decision to throw a party to sell slinky underwear. Offred was shocked at the idea, but Moira said older women liked it, to beat the competition of the Pornomarts.

Offred tries to understand what life was like back then. She remembers it as a combination of the ordinary and the grotesque, with stories in the papers about sexual attacks and murders. But people back then tended to ignore the grotesque; those stories were about women in the papers, not ordinary lives.

She remarks on the neighborhood's quietness and goes to sit on the window seat. It has a cushion embroidered with the word FAITH, the only word she has to read. Outside she sees Nick open the car door for the Commander. If she could spit, she thinks, or drop something from the window, she could hit the Commander's head. This reminds her of how Moira and she once dropped water bombs from the window of their college dorm. As the Commander leaves in the car, Offred realizes she doesn't feel hatred for this man, but rather an emotion far more complicated.

Analysis

Offred's recollection of Moira's underwhore party and of the Pornomarts suggest that the pre-Gilead society had become increasingly sexually permissive. In addition, sexual violence against women had become almost commonplace. Her memories of reading about this violence in the papers is a reminder of why many people accepted the Republic of Gilead at its start. Things had gotten out of hand, and many were willing to accept limits to their freedom if it meant they would be safe. But Gilead's executions show that its people's surrender of their freedoms did not end violence; Gilead has merely made violence a tool of the state.

Offred's realization that she doesn't hate the Commander echoes her ambiguous feelings for the Guardians. She doesn't know how to label her complicated feelings for him, although she's certain it is not love.

Chapter 11

New Character:

An unnamed doctor

Summary

Offred tells of her latest monthly visit to her doctor. It is his job to make sure his Handmaid patients are in good health so they can bear children. During the examination, he whispers, "I can help you," adding, "I've helped others." Clearly he is telling Offred that he can get her pregnant. He adds that most Commanders are sterile, so if she really wants a baby, his way is the only real one.

Offred is shocked, since in Gilead it is forbidden to suggest that males may be sterile; only women may be sterile or infertile. She's shocked, too, because what the doctor proposes could mean death for both of them if they are caught.

Yet, she is aware of the doctor's power over her: he could declare her sterile, which would mean she would become a doomed Unwoman. No one would question the doctor's verdict.

She also is terrified simply by the idea of choice. It has been so long since she was faced with choices; at the Red Center the whole idea of choice was supposed to have been erased from Handmaids' lives. She backs away from the opportunity, claiming "It's too dangerous." But the doctor encourages her to think about it and to accept the offer the next month.

Analysis

The fact that the doctor's nurse carries a gun in a shoulder holster in the office shows that the population program involving the Handmaids is important to the regime and therefore well protected. The doctor is likely a key player in Gilead's forces, but his subversive words to Offred—that most Commanders are sterile so why not let him get her pregnant?—shows how the rules and beliefs of the society are easily dismissed by those in power.

That male sterility is a taboo subject, and that only women can be infertile, shows Gilead's misogyny: only women are at fault; they deserve to be treated as they are.

Chapter 12

Summary

Preparing for her bath, Offred is uncomfortable with her nakedness because she is not used to the sight of her own body, and because that is what Gilead has reduced her to: just a body, whose only purpose is as a womb for Commanders' babies.

Lying in the bath, she remembers when her infant daughter, in the child's seat of a grocery cart, was stolen by a desperate, childless woman while Offred was at the cat food section. The woman was arrested and the baby restored. That kidnapping was an act of madness; the second kidnapping was an act of Gilead law.

She remembers her daughter at age five, when they were separated, and the photographs and other mementos she once had of the little girl, who would be eight now, she thinks.

She looks at the tattoo on her ankle—four numbers and the picture of an eye—the symbol of Gilead's secret police. Clearly this is her permanent ID number.

Then she emerges from her bath and dresses. Her wet hair reminds her of old news footage of women having their heads shaved, kneeling in the center of an angry crowd.

Cora brings her supper tray, the usual nutritious but boring food, and she eats methodically, without enjoyment. She saves the pat of butter, hiding it in the toe of a shoe. Then she composes herself and waits.

Analysis

The theft of Offred's baby in the store by a deranged woman probably stemmed from the scarcity of children in pre-Gilead society, which helped prompt the revolution.

Offred's sense of alienation from her body shows the effectiveness of her indoctrination. Denied the companionship of others and forced to wear garments that hide her face and body, she cannot even feel comfortable with her own body. The tattoo on her ankle, both her ID and a means of preventing her escape, echoes the Nazi practice of tattooing its concentration camp inmates with ID numbers, again linking Gilead with the worst examples of inhumanity.

Her memory of the women whose heads were shaven must be from an old TV documentary. During 1944 and 1945, in newly liberated cities in Western Europe, women who had consorted with German troops were marched to public squares, forced to kneel, and had their heads shaved. Since the fashion for women of the time was to have long hair, this head shaving was humiliating for women and marked them for months afterward as outcasts and collaborators with the Nazi enemy.

Study Questions

1. Why was Offred's daughter taken from her?

2. Why does Offred wish her story were untrue?

3. Why do Econowives hate Handmaids?

4. What might be the consequences of Gilead's persecution of Catholic priests?

5. Why is Offred upset at seeing the Commander outside her door?

6. Why does Offred feel the need to invent a face and a personality for her predecessor?

7. What is the significance of Offred remembering the song "Amazing Grace"?

8. When she watches the Commander from her bedroom window, why does Offred remember dropping water bombs at college?

9. Why does the doctor offer to get Offred pregnant?

10. Why are Handmaids tattooed on the ankle?

Answers

1. Most women in Gilead are childless, including Wives, so children are prized. Therefore, a Wife's acquisition of a child is a boon for her and a sign of prestige. Besides, since Wives are not allowed to work, having a child gives them some-

thing to fill their days with. Since Handmaids are stripped of their names and all their individuality, and must be abject servants of the state, losing their children is an absolutely necessary part of this process.

2. Toying with the idea of the truth or untruth of her story, Offred is desperate for any kind of escape. She knows that her future in Gilead is bleak at best, and at worst she may soon lose her life. Telling herself that her present situation is a product of her imagination, or just a bad dream, is the most readily available means of escape. But if Offred loses the ability to distinguish reality from hallucination, she will sink into insanity, and Gilead is not likely to treat the insane with compassion; it probably kills them. Further, Offred's sanity is vital to any escape attempt.

3. Econowives have very low status in Gilead, as their name implies ("economy grade" is the lowest grade for groceries). They are assigned husbands, whom they have to serve. Although they are not allowed individualism, Handmaids have status as the potential saviors of Gilead through their ability to have babies, and they have nothing but free time on their hands. So Econowives envy them. But we have seen that Offred would give anything to keep busy like the Econowives. Envy and hatred between different sectors of Gilead society helps keep the regime in place.

4. Of all the religious and racial persecutions Gilead undertakes, slaughtering Catholic priests is probably the most incendiary. Latin America, from which Gilead gets many of its foods and raw materials, is overwhelmingly Catholic, and this policy will not be well received in those countries. Perhaps this is a major reason why Central America is at war with Gilead. Catholicism is the major religion of many European countries as well, so Gilead's policy undoubtedly is creating enemies there. Finally, the Catholic church has experienced persecution in many parts of the world at different times, and has learned ways of fighting back, or at least surviving. Catholicism was a central force in the Polish resistance to Communism, and helped to precipitate the col-

lapse of the Soviet empire, so it could well do the same to Gilead.

5. Gilead separates its different categories of people except under certain rigidly controlled circumstances. Even within a Commander's household, as we will learn, there are strict rules about who can be where and when, even for Commanders. That the Commander has broken one of those rules upsets Offred, who wonders, quite naturally, if this might endanger her.

6. Deprived of family and friends, and living among hostile people, Offred is desperate for companionship. Her fantasies about her predecessor, even down to the freckles, are like the creation of imaginary playmates by lonely children: it fills a human need. Like all people, Offred needs someone to act as a companion and confidant.

7. It is significant that Offred recalls the song "Amazing Grace" because its message is important to the book. Perhaps the fact that it was written by the former captain of a slave ship, who experienced a conversion and repented for having worked at such an inhuman trade, helps Atwood hint at a possible conversion in Gilead. But Offred can translate the message of the hymn of spiritual liberation into a message of physical liberation, too: "I once was lost but now am found" certainly is something she yearns to experience. If only Luke could find her! The hymn may play the same role for her as spirituals played in the lives of slaves: a coded message expressing their deepest desires for freedom.

8. Just as Offred has invented an imaginary "playmate" out of her predecessor, a kind of reversion to childhood, she, too, imagines performing a childish antic toward the Commander. After all, Handmaids are like children: all decisions are made for them by an "adult," including what they wear and eat, even when they have a bath, so it is natural that they sometimes act and think childishly.

9. The doctor may be compassionate toward Offred and his other Handmaid patients, offering the only way he has to

save them. Or he may simply be a lecher, enjoying having sex with as many young women as he can.

10. Since the Handmaids wear ankle-length gowns and Guardians are barely allowed to look them in the face at the check points, it is completely unlikely that a Guardian would ever see a Handmaid's tattooed ID. More likely it is there for the Handmaids themselves to see, yet another reminder that they are just numbers, not human beings.

Suggested Essay Topics

1. Consider the naming of the Handmaids—Offred, Ofwarren, and Ofglen, for example. What does this reveal about the values and power dynamics of Gilead? What parallels can be made between the naming system of their society and the naming of women in our society?

2. Each category of women in Gilead is resentful of the others. Explain the reasons for this resentment and discuss its ultimate effect.

3. How does Gilead's policing of language help to control the thoughts of its citizens? For example, why is Offred so shocked when her doctor uses the word "sterile" in reference to men?

SECTION SIX

Part V: Nap

Chapter 13

Summary

Remembering when she could walk through art galleries, Offred recalls certain nineteenth-century paintings of Oriental harems, calling them pictures of "suspended animation, about waiting," precisely what her life is now.

This reminds her of reading about "pig balls," toys made for pigs to play with, to overcome their boredom as they are fattened for the slaughter. She also remembers learning in a college psychology course about rats that would give themselves electric shocks to have something to do. Clearly, she can relate to both of these.

She wonders if the Handmaid-trainees at the Red Center were drugged to make them so lethargic. How else could they have endured the boredom, all that waiting?

This reminds her of Moira's arrival at the Red Center, three weeks after Offred's arrival, and the boost it had given her. They had managed several secret, whispered conversations in the toilets, Offred's first real communication since her capture.

Lying down on the hooked rug to nap, she thinks again about her body, which she once commanded: what to do, where to go, etc. Now it defines her: only it, not she, has purpose.

Half-asleep, she dreams of Luke, but he won't look at her and

doesn't seem to hear her. She reminds herself that he may be dead.

Then she dreams about her daughter and the two of them flee-ing through underbrush with the child drugged so she will not cry out. There are sounds of shots behind them and they fall to the ground, and Offred shelters the child with her own body. But the dream grows dark, and she is watching her daughter being carried away.

Then a bell wakes her.

Analysis

Moira's appearance at the Red Center is surprising. Such an ardent feminist seems like a prime candidate for exile to the Colo-nies.

Moira brings Offred hope for two reasons, first as solid con-tact with Offred's past life, and second, because she is a habitual rebel, so perhaps she will find a way to resist—or better yet, es-cape from—the Center, with Offred. Offred wants nothing more than to escape from the Center so she can try again to find her daughter and husband.

Offred's dreams of her husband and child, and her obsession with her loss of control over her body and of her life's direction, show how central these are to her. But there are no "pig balls" for Handmaids, only boredom and waiting.

Part VI: Household

Chapter 14

Summary

Summoned by the bell, Offred reports to the living room. The furniture reeks of money—rugs, paintings, for example—that reflect Serena Joy's insistence on quality mixed with sentimentality. Offred thinks she would like to steal something from this room, to give her a small sense of power, and to thumb her nose at her jailers.

The two Marthas join her, then Nick, who stands so close behind her that the toe of his boot touches her foot. Serena Joy hobbles slowly down the stairs, her cane tapping; she enters and sits down, the only one who may sit.

Serena Joy clicks the television from one channel to another, most of them blank, one of them a jammed broadcast from Montréal, until she finds the news, which shows a battle in the Appalachians, and a prisoner held by two Angels. Gilead TV, Offred reminds herself, only shows victories. She wonders if this is a real prisoner or merely an actor. The TV anchor tells of the capture of members of a Quaker ring smuggling refugees to Canada. Two Quakers, a man and a woman, are shown, looking terrified. The next news item is from Detroit and shows African Americans who are being shipped to National Homeland One in North Dakota. Then Serena Joy turns off the set and they wait for the Commander.

Waiting, Offred holds her real name in her mind like a secret treasure, and remembers how she and Luke attempted to escape to Canada, pretending to their daughter that they were merely going for a picnic in the country.

Analysis

Offred's suspicions that the television news may be fake, and displayed prisoners may be actors, show what can take place where there is no free press. News becomes so one-sided that it is no longer believed. Her comment on the jammed signal from Montréal bears this out: only regimes that fear the truth will block signals from other countries.

The Appalachian battle shows that Gilead has enemies far closer to its New England heartland than those in Florida and California, while the Quaker prisoners are a clear sign that a new underground railroad, like that of slavery times, truly exists—another means of undermining Gilead.

The evacuation of the "Children of Ham" from Detroit and elsewhere to "homelands" in North Dakota is particularly chilling. Noah cursed his son Ham and all his line, to be "hewers of wood and drawers of water"—servants and slaves. Tradition has these Children of Ham as Africans, and South Africa's former Apartheid regime used this to justify depriving non-white South Africans of their rights. Many American racists also have used this biblical text to justify their abuse of African-Americans. That Gilead has revived this term is a clear sign that this is a racist regime.

The deportation to "homelands" is also reminiscent of Apartheid South Africa's exiling many black citizens to "Bantustans": agricultural wastelands, with too many people crowded onto arid land, without proper health care or other facilities.

The Nazis spoke of "relocating" Jews, Slavs, and other unwanted peoples to new locations for their own peace and prosperity. But, in fact, they were "resettled" as slave laborers or exterminated.

Nick's placing himself so close behind Offred that their feet touch is another sign that he ignores Gilead's rules. Or is he trying to provoke her? Her safest course is to say nothing.

Chapter 15

Summary

The Commander knocks at the living room door, for this officially is Serena Joy's territory, but he enters without waiting for permission.

Offred remarks that he looks like a retired Midwestern banker or a man who might have appeared in a vodka ad, except for his black uniform. His mild and distracted air is surprising. She wonders what it is like to be in his position: Fine? Hellish?

The Commander unlocks a leather-covered box, taking out a Bible. He reads God's words to Adam in Genesis: "Be fruitful, and multiply, and replenish the earth . . . ." Then he reads the story of Rachel and Leah, which was read to the Handmaid-trainees every morning at the Center.

At the Center, the Beatitudes were read to them during lunch, but a significant addition, "Blessed are the silent," is slipped in among the Beatitudes.

And she remembers Moira's plans for escaping the Red Center by inducing a case of scurvy, as she told Offred.

Now Offred notices that Serena Joy is crying and remarks that she always does this on "the night of the Ceremony."

She recalls Moira being carried out of the Center to an ambulance, the first step in her escape attempt. But that evening Moira was dragged into the Center by two Aunts. She had been beaten with steel cables on the soles of her feet and could not walk for a week. As Aunt Lydia remarked, Handmaids don't need their hands and feet.

The Commander clears his throat and stands, signaling that the session is over.

Analysis

Serena Joy's "ruling" the living room is another example of how Gilead divides its people. Locking up the Bible between the sessions is reminiscent of pre-Reformation days when only the clergy had access to the Bible, lest the laity read it and give it their own

interpretations. It is ironic that access to the Bible is so limited, since Gilead pretends to be based entirely on it.

Offred's memory of Bible readings at the Center shows again that Gilead tinkers with the Scriptures whenever it suits its purpose.

Moira's beating demonstrates Gilead's brutal side, especially towards women. That hands and feet can be savaged, even permanently crippled, is evidence that a Handmaid is merely a walking womb, and wombs don't need to walk.

The Commander's rather bland appearance bears out the idea that evil need not appear horrible. The social critic Hannah Arendt, in her study of Nazism, wrote of "the banality of evil," the idea that the most ordinary-seeming people may be capable of brutal and inhuman acts. This bland-looking Commander has helped create a society in which, among other things, women are beaten mercilessly and "enemies" are executed and hung out for public display.

Chapter 16

Summary

After the Bible session, the Commander, Serena Joy, and Offred retire to the Commander and Serena Joy's bedroom. Serena Joy lies on the four-poster bed, and Offred lies between her legs, her head on Serena Joy's abdomen, and her raised arms held with her skirt raised to her waist. Then the Commander attempts to inseminate her. This is the Ceremony.

Offred feels as if her mind and body are no longer linked. At least this Commander, she muses, does not smell as bad as her previous one.

Once the Commander ejaculates, he leaves the room and Serena Joy, releasing Offred's hands, tells her to go, though regulations require that after the Ceremony the Handmaid remain lying down for 10 minutes to increase the chances of pregnancy.

Analysis

The Ceremony, with its fake "togetherness" of Handmaid and Wife, is at the center of Gilead life: "Be fruitful and multiply." It is humiliating to all three participants. While the Commander and Offred endure it by letting their minds drift away, apparently Serena Joy is filled with hatred; she cannot bear the sight of Offred.

Offred claims that the act could not be called a rape since she chose to become a Handmaid rather than being shipped out to the Colonies. But since that was really not a legitimate choice and since the sex act is clearly not consensual, it can be regarded as a ritual rape.

Chapter 17

Summary

In her room after the Ceremony, Offred takes the pat of butter from her shoe and rubs it into her face as a substitute for skin cream, which the Wives have outlawed for Handmaids. Offred regards using this substitute skin cream as a gesture of hope, a statement that this captivity will end and she will want to feel attractive again.

She lies on her bed, desperately missing Luke, wishing she could be in his arms and feel loved. Then she quietly goes down to the living room, a forbidden act. What she wants is to steal something, anything, as an act of defiance, a way of thumbing her nose at the Ceremony. She will steal one of the dying daffodils, she thinks.

Suddenly she realizes she is not alone. Nick is there in the dark, which is also forbidden. He pulls her to him and kisses her. Then they draw apart and he tells her the Commander wants to see her in his office the next night. When she asks him why, he doesn't say. Troubled, she returns to her room.

Analysis

Although the Ceremony is distasteful to all three participants, the Commander has helped set the rules for it, so he has some

control of things, while his Wife will gain a baby if it is successful. But Offred is a total victim of the Ceremony.

Afterwards she needs to commit some act of defiance to recover some sense of self. But she is not ready to accept meaningless martyrdom. Stealing a wilted flower is defiant, but safe.

Nick's presence in the living room and his kissing her add to his mystery. Is he tempting Offred in order to betray her? Or is he a kindred soul, a fellow rebel? Offred's desire to go beyond just a kiss is perhaps because she needs to expunge the ritual rape of the Ceremony with a sexual act that she *chooses*.

Nick's message that the Commander wants to see her the following night, though, is startling, and Offred is thrown into confusion again.

Part VII: Night

Chapter 18

Summary

In bed, Offred remembers lying pregnant beside Luke, with him feeling the movements of their unborn child. She is overwhelmed now by the absence of love in her life; it is the ultimate deprivation. She is a "missing person" in both senses: missing from the people and place she belongs to, and filled with a sense of missing—Luke, their child, and love.

She wonders about Luke's fate and sees one vision after another: Luke lying dead in the woods where they were discovered; Luke ill in some wretched prison; Luke having escaped, involved in a government in exile, and planning her escape from Gilead. Which one is true, she wonders. She believes in all three simultaneously.

She remembers a gravestone she has seen since first coming to the Commander's house, with the words "In hope" inscribed on it. Does Luke hope, she wonders.

Analysis

Of the three versions of Luke she conjures up, the worst for Offred is that of him in prison—beaten, ill, the youth knocked out of him. She would prefer him dead. The best version is of him free and planning her rescue. Yet it seems the least concrete. She *sees* him dead, right down to the number of bullet holes; she *sees* him in prison, even to a cut on his neck. But she does not *see* him safe, among friends, planning her escape.

So while Offred tells herself to hope, it seems her hope is running out, at least as far as Luke is concerned. Perhaps her summons to the Commander's office has weakened her hope.

Study Questions

1. Why doesn't Gilead give Handmaids "pig balls" to pass the time?

2. Why does Offred increasingly dream of Luke and her child?

3. What does Moira mean to Offred?

4. The TV news is meant to show Gilead's successes. Why does Offred manage to take comfort from it?

5. Why is Gilead transporting African Americans to "homelands" in remote areas?

6. Why are parts of the house the Commander's and other parts Serena Joy's?

7. Why is the Ceremony likely to be unsuccessful?

8. What does the hidden pat of butter mean to Offred?

9. Why does Nick kiss Offred?

10. Why does Offred begin thinking of Luke and wondering about his whereabouts after the events of this evening?

Answers

1. Gilead probably denies Handmaids the equivalent of "pig balls" to remind them of their place. But all creatures need stimulation, as the pigs and rats show, to maintain their well-being. Depressed and unfit women are less likely to conceive and go on to bear healthy children than physically fit, happy ones. Mind and body interact, so Gilead's divorce of the two is not likely to help increase the birth rate.

2. Offred's dreams of Luke and their child are haunting ones of them dying or disappearing. They suggest that Offred is

sinking into despair and her chances of survival are waning.

3.   Moira is all that Offred is not: physically and emotionally strong—going her own way at whatever the cost. She is a role model for Offred. She is also Offred's closest friend.

4.   Although the news shows rebels defeated and Quakers of the new underground railroad under arrest, it does show that both of these things exist, and the fight goes on. The existence of organized resistance to Gilead helps boost Offred's will to resist.

5.   Gilead was created by whites to correct the decline in the white birthrate. It is essentially racist, exiling African Americans and Jews, and probably others who don't fit their pattern.

6.   With its emphasis on the family, it seems odd that husbands and wives have separate territories in their homes. Perhaps it stems from the presence of a Handmaid in the house and the resulting hostility between husband and wife. Or, since Gilead is ruled by men, and organized around state prostitution (i.e., the Handmaid system), perhaps the Commanders have divided their homes in this way to see as little of the Wives as possible.

7.   The Handmaids are demoralized, and the only exercise they ever get is an occasional walk to the store. The Commanders are in their 50s and 60s, maybe older, with a declining libido. The Ceremony happens only once a month. The circumstances for the Ceremony are anything but relaxed. All of these facts together virtually ensure failure, if the aim is a high birthrate.

8.   The butter, Offred's substitute for face cream, gives her a tiny sense of normalcy, a reminder of when she had nice shampoos and hair conditioners, body lotions, and face creams to pamper her body and make her feel attractive. Even butter is better than nothing. This act of applying the butter— what Offred calls a private ceremony—also helps to support her hope that she will some day escape from her circumstances and will be touched again, in love or desire.

9. Guardians, as shown earlier, can scarcely even look at Handmaids, and cannot talk to them except on official business. Touching them is forbidden. So Nick, if he is not an *agent provocateur,* is either desperate for a woman or a kind of male Moira, prepared to risk his life rather than knuckle under to the Gilead system.

10. It is likely Offred's thoughts turn to Luke because of her brief entanglement with Nick. Since she doesn't know if Luke is dead or alive, she seems to feel guilty over her possible infidelity. Her sexual involvement with the Commander during the Ceremony probably does not evoke feelings of guilt since that was not consensual sex.

Suggested Essay Topics

1. Offred and Moira are very different people. Outline these differences and discuss what may nevertheless make them friends. What does their friendship do for the novel?

2. Offred's narration is made up of a confusing mix of details from the present tense action of the novel and details from her various memories of the past. In what ways are her memories connected to what is happening to her at the Commander's house? Why has Atwood chosen a narrative style that so frequently blurs distinctions between present and past?

Part VIII: Birth Day

Chapter 19

Summary

Offred dreams that she awakens in her former home and opens the bedroom door to find her daughter running toward her, open-armed. She wonders if this, and dreams like it, are just dreams, or if perhaps it's her present life that is the dream, a nightmare from which she'll soon awaken. But she fights the temptation to believe her present life is the unreal one, for her sanity tells her otherwise, and her sanity is the one thing she still possesses.

Awake, she sees the FAITH cushion and speculates that there must have been companions embroidered with HOPE and CHARITY, but what has become of them? Perhaps Serena Joy, ever neat and thrifty, has put them in Rita's and Cora's rooms.

Then, another bland breakfast arrives. While Offred eats, the Birthmobile van arrives, and Cora summons her. Seated in the Birthmobile, she asks who is to give birth. It is Ofwarren—Janine.

Offred remembers that the chances of a healthy baby are only one in four. Radiation, toxicity of air and water, and chemicals in food have taken their toll on human reproduction. Offred remembers the school desk at the Center where she sat during Aunt Lydia's talks on the fertility problem. It was etched with messages, *"J.H. loves B.P."*, for example, which summoned up the world of adolescent dating and love, things that ceased to exist years ago. Now there is no love, and sex is regulated by the state.

The red Birthmobile van arrives at Ofwarren's house, and Offred notes the Emerge van parked down the street, in which doctors wait. Doctors are not allowed at births in Gilead unless there is risk.

Another vehicle arrives, a blue Birthmobile, reserved for Wives, much more comfortable than the Handmaids' one.

Offred wonders how Ofwarren was treated during her pregnancy and what she was thinking as she awaited the birth of the child that would earn her a favored place in Gilead. But if the child isn't viable, she could become an Unwoman and be exiled to the Colonies to die. It is a crapshoot with bad odds—one to four—and Janine's life is the stake.

Analysis

Offred's temptation to see her happy dreams of the past as reality and her present situation as nightmare shows she is beginning to lose her grip and must steel herself not to slide any further into despair or madness. If she loses her sanity, Gilead has won.

The cushion, with its word FAITH, may once have been part of a set of three. In Corinthians the Apostle Paul speaks of faith, hope, and charity as the heart of religious life, ending this letter to Christians in Corinth: "And now abideth faith, hope, charity, these three; but the greatest of these is charity."

If this cushion was part of a trio, FAITH, HOPE and CHARITY, it is very significant that the others have disappeared. As Offred has shown, there is no hope in Gilead, and the regime shows no charity, and no compassion. So Gilead has gutted Christianity.

The gathering of Handmaids and Wives, via their two classes of Birthmobiles, shows a new side of Gilead's women's world. Birth is celebrated only by women; men are excluded. The doctors, parked a discreet distance away, as if they were stamped "For emergency use only," are a vivid statement.

Certainly, as far as sisterhood goes, though, the two classes of women are hardly united. The Wives' treat the woman giving birth as they might treat something that is not quite a household pet, but rather a necessary evil ("Little whores, all of them," Offred imagines a Wife saying).

Aunt Lydia's lectures on the falling birthrate (apparently only among Caucasians) due to increasing levels of pollution, are pretty accurate predictions of the future. Since the novel was published, there have been many reports of a dramatic drop in sperm counts among men throughout the world.

Chapter 20

Summary

Inside Ofwarren's house, Offred notices a splendid array of food laid out for the Wives—pastries, fruit, coffee, and wine—while the Handmaids will make do with sandwiches and milk.

In the master bedroom, the Handmaids gather in a circle around an old-fashioned birthing stool. But this one is different: it has a second, raised seat attached behind it, obviously for the Wife to sit in while Ofwarren sits in the lower stool to give birth.

Offred remembers Aunt Lydia's saying, "From each according to her ability; to each according to his need." She also recalls cautionary movies shown at the Red Center, vicious pornography from earlier times and one film about Unwomen and their revolutionary feminism (although Aunt Lydia remarks, "some of their ideas were sound enough"). In that film Offred glimpsed her own mother holding a sign saying "TAKE BACK THE NIGHT," while others carried pro-choice signs. She is startled at how young her mother looked.

This reminds her of the way her mother used to criticize her for being "just a backlash" and how she used to goad Luke. Offred thinks, "She expected me to vindicate her life for her," but Offred wanted to live her own life and make her own choices. All the same, she misses her mother deeply.

Analysis

The birthing stool is an ancient device that has long since been replaced by the hospital maternity table. In recent times, there has been a movement to replace the obstetrician with the once

honored midwife in all except complicated births, with the woman delivering her baby in her own home, in her own bed, often with her family present.

Gilead is turning its back on modern medicine (ultrasound is now illegal) to feminize the birth process and to return to ancient ways. As in so much else, Gilead picks and chooses from past and present almost at whim.

The extra seat on the birthing stool fits in with the Ceremony: Wife and Handmaid symbolically are one—though we have learned that, far from being united, they really are enemies.

Aunt Lydia's "from each according to her ability" is not from the Bible, as she says, but from the 1848 *Communist Manifesto* of Marx and Engels. It's another example of Gilead's fiddling with the Bible.

The Red Center films that link the vilest pornography with pro-choice feminists are part of Gilead's brainwashing process.

Offred's insistence despite her mother's wishes that she go her own way and choose her own life perhaps bodes well for her managing to hold out against Gilead.

Chapter 21

Summary

With the bedroom full of women—25 or so—and with its windows closed despite the heat of early summer, Offred feels oppressed as she and the others coach Janine with her breathing. Janine is having trouble with the delivery. She is restless and does not seem to know where she is or what she is doing.

Finally, it's time. Janine is placed on the stool and the Wife hurries to sit behind her. The baby is born, and Aunt Elizabeth from the Center inspects it: it is apparently a healthy girl, not a "shredder." Relief and happiness engulf the room, and the wall between Wives and Handmaids is lowered briefly. The Wife chooses the baby's name: Angela.

As for Janine, whether she has another child or not, she is safe

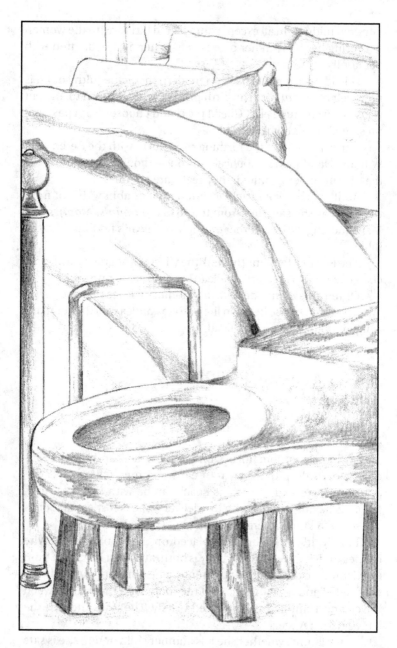

from doom in the Colonies, if Angela proves to be healthy.

Offred feels exhausted, and her breasts ache and leak in sympathy with Janine.

Yet, the chapter ends with a wry note as Offred thinks, regarding her mother, "You wanted a women's culture. Well, now there is one. It isn't what you meant, but it exists."

Analysis

Although the Wife shares the birthing stool with Janine, there is no doubt who is in charge: the Wife is the one who names *her* baby. Although Janine will nurse the child for the next few months, she will not be allowed to mother it.

Offred's comments that Gilead's emphasis on birthing has created "a woman's culture." This is something feminists like her mother called for, though they certainly would have condemned this particular form of culture. It is deeply ironic that the exclusionary tactics taken by radical feminists in the formulation of their agenda are echoed in the state-regulated structure of Gilead.

Chapter 22

Summary

Again at home, Offred says she is too exhausted to continue her story. Instead, she muses about the illicit grapevine, messages passed from one Handmaid to another and the fact that, even in Gilead, there are alliances.

This reminds her of Moira's escape from the Red Center. Moira blocked a toilet so it overflowed, and reported the overflow to Aunt Elizabeth, who went with Moira to inspect it. In the stall, Moira poked Aunt Elizabeth from behind with something sharp, telling her to be quiet or die. She swapped clothes with Aunt Elizabeth and tied her up. Then she marched out the front door, past the Angels, to freedom. Her weapon was the metal lever inside the toilet, hardly lethal. Her real weapon was bluff.

The escape excited the other Handmaids enormously: the idea

that the system could be beaten had only been a theory until then.

Analysis

Moira has often criticized Offred for being too timid and passive. The story of Moira's escape bolsters this idea: Moira achieves liberty while Offred stays a prisoner. And it isn't Moira's physical strength that gets her out; it's her nerve. For the moment, that seems to be the message: dare!

Chapter 23

Summary

Offred states, "I intend to get out of here," adding that others have, but hinting that many of them escaped only through suicide.

She complains of the difficulty of keeping her story straight, keeping things in their right order, and getting them accurate, since, after all, she can't write it down. She muses on what the whole struggle of Gilead is really about.

When she wakes the morning after the birth, she is told by Cora that the baby is indeed a keeper, and Cora shyly suggests, "Maybe we have one soon." Offred thinks Cora wants a birth in the house because of the festivity and the chance to take care of a child.

Just after nine that evening, Offred anxiously goes downstairs toward the Commander's office, wondering what awaits her. She knocks at the door and is told to enter.

What lies inside is so ordinary—desk, chair, fireplace—that it is an anticlimax. The Commander leans his elbow on the mantel, again reminding Offred of a picture in a glossy men's magazine. His casualness is too fake. He tells her to sit down, then seats himself in the leather chair behind the desk. He says he wants them to play Scrabble together. Offred holds herself rigid and expressionless, but shows she's willing to play.

She thinks, though, that Scrabble is a game for old people, or for rainy days at the summer cottage. She realizes now that it is forbidden fruit, requiring a capacity not merely to read and write,

but to remember the most difficult words. She wins the first game with words like "larynx," "valance," "quince," and "zygote," but lets the Commander win the second. Before she leaves, the Commander asks her to kiss him.

Surprise, pity, and rage boil up in her. She is his victim, his possession, yet he has also shown a weakness in wanting her, and she feels sorry for him. But she realizes that she is powerless in this situation so she kisses him, then leaves.

Analysis

Newborn babies in this society are referred to as "keepers" or "shredders," depending on their viability. This terminology makes them sound more like fish or files of paper, than human beings. It also indicates the number of malformed babies.

This game of Scrabble is a subversive act. This word game is illegal for Offred; being alone with the Commander, unchaperoned, is illegal; even her being downstairs at night breaks rules. So why has he had her do this and risk her life? And why does she agree to it?

Since the Commander has helped write Gilead's laws, he, above all, should obey them. Perhaps he is merely a hypocrite, or perhaps he likes the risk of living on the edge.

Offred, with her pity for him, seems to think that he, too, is a victim, another lonely person desperate to reach out and make human contact. It seems everybody in Gilead, from top to bottom, is a victim of this society. To endure it, people have to break the rules sometimes.

It is ironic that the Commander, who regularly has intercourse with Offred, should shyly ask for a kiss. But the sex is a ritual dictated by the state; the kiss is a private act between individuals. What complicates this kiss, however, is that it is not based on mutual desire; one individual still has power over the other.

SECTION TEN

Part IX: Night

Chapter 24

Summary

Back in her room, still in her Handmaid gown, Offred sits in the dark trying to get perspective on what has just happened, and on her whole present life. She tells herself she must live in the present, not in memories or hope for the future. But her experience with the Commander has changed things.

Aunt Lydia used to imply that men are just sex machines, so women must learn to manipulate them. Yet the Commander's vulnerability confounds her.

She remembers a television documentary about a Nazi death camp, composed of interviews with survivors from both sides. One was the camp Commander's mistress. Dying of emphysema, yet carefully made up, she insisted that the Commander was human, a decent man. According to the program, she committed suicide soon after the interview.

Preparing for bed, Offred has an irresistible urge to laugh, so she crawls into the closet with her hands against her mouth to hold back the laughter.

Analysis

Obviously, Offred identifies with the woman in the documentary who finds excuses for the death-camp commander as she is seeking to explain the Commander's behavior. Both men have committed evil, both are commanders, yet both are human. Denying either their evil or their humanity is false. Yet, it is hard to accept that these exist in the same person. How do you fight someone who is evil *and* human?

Perhaps it is this absurd conflict of emotions that prompts her laughing fit. Or perhaps it is the absurdity of the Scrabble game, the two of them playing like naughty children fooling their parents.

Offred feels that her life has been changed, for her involvement with the Commander allows her some small degree of choice and power. While she knows she cannot refuse him his bizarre requests, she also realizes she can manipulate the situation to ask for something in return.

Study Questions

1. The chances that Ofwarren will deliver a healthy baby are only one in four. What does this indicate about the state of the environment?

2. Since they play no real role in the birth process, why do the Wives and Handmaids all attend the birth of Ofwarren's/Janine's child?

3. Since the birth is a special women's event, why are the Handmaids given inferior food to that of the Wives?

4. Offred notes that all machines that could tell the viability of a fetus have been outlawed in Gilead. What does this reveal about the society?

5. Why are the Handmaid trainees at the Center shown films of pro-choice feminist rallies after having viewed violent pornography?

6. How could Offred have vindicated her mother?

7. If birthing babies is Gilead's chief goal, why are the babies spoken of so callously?

8. Of all the games he could choose, why does the Commander want to play Scrabble?

9. Why does the Commander ask Offred to kiss him?

10. Why is it significant that Offred recalls a documentary featuring the mistress of a commander from the Nazi concentration camps after her "date" with the Commander of her household?

Answers

1. The low birth rate and the high infant mortality rate suggest that the environment has become increasingly toxic. Concern about pollution seems to have been another factor that lead to the Gilead revolution. Offred provides some of the details of the ecological crisis by referring to exploding atomic power plants along the San Andreas fault and a mutant strain of syphilis that could not be cured.

2. Gilead is supposed to be about "family values"—some of them, at least—and it intends to stop the decline in white births. So the birth of Janine's child is not just a family event, but a community celebration. But Gilead segregates the sexes, giving most of its world to men, but leaving some for women. This is one of those areas.

3. Gilead is full of fraud. It claims to be Bible-based, yet it adds to or deletes from the Bible as it chooses. It also gives a very literal interpretation of many passages. Gilead is divided into many hostile groups. So even at this "women's festival" there is still division and hostility.

4. The banning of ultrasounds shows Gilead's absolute restriction against abortion. Since no pregnancy can be terminated, there is no need to monitor the health of the fetus. This also illustrates the society's desperate need for children since every fetus is taken to full term. But by removing this element of prenatal care—in the same way that the doctors in the Emerge van are excluded from the birthing room in all but critical cases—the regime is denying women the medical intervention that could ensure more healthy babies.

5. Linking pornography with the feminists is part of Gilead's manipulation of truth. It is a form of aversion therapy in

which something the subject likes is linked to something she dislikes, until she ends up disliking both. Gilead cares about manipulation, not about truth, and, since it is prepared to manipulate the Bible, it is equally prepared to manipulate the truth.

6. If Offred had been a feminist leader, her mother would have been vindicated. Her mother chose to have a child without a husband. She talked repeatedly of feminism, disparaged men and marriage, and involved her child in her causes and rallies. When Offred chose a more traditional route to creating a family, her mother felt that her own life choices were not being justified and were perhaps even being questioned.

7. Speaking of babies as "shredders" (who shreds them, and how?) shows the real indifference to human life in Gilead. It is like those people who profess to believe in humanity but are vile to individual human beings. The one thing Gilead seems to despise is love or compassion. So it's in keeping with the whole mood of Gilead that babies are spoken of so callously.

8. Checkers, Clue, and a hundred other games would be less provocative than Scrabble. Since it is a game of letters and spelling, which are taboo for Handmaids, it is more daring than any other game. The only other game that would approach it is Monopoly, which is about the acquisition of property and money, since Handmaids can acquire nothing. Clearly the Commander wants to play the most dangerous game he can with Offred.

9. Kissing Offred is another of the Commander's dangerous games, and perhaps this is the only reason he wants to. But he may also crave some real human contact with a woman, since he has none with his Wife. Perhaps he is almost as lonely as Offred.

10. Offred realizes she is moving into a complicitous relationship with her oppressor and this troubles her. The mistress featured in the documentary denied knowing about the ovens and claimed her lover was not a monster. Offred doesn't have the choice to refuse her Commander's advances as

perhaps did this mistress, but she still must deal with the ambiguity of seeing the humanity of the Commander at the same time that she despises what he represents. The fact that the mistress committed suicide shortly after the making of the documentary also connects her to Offred, who continues to see suicide as the only means of escape.

Suggested Essay Topics

1. Offred and her mother made different choices for themselves in terms of love and family. Compare their choices. Also, consider the way Offred was affected by her upbringing, both during her pre-Gilead life and during her life as a Handmaid.

2. Discuss what the Scrabble game means to the Commander as opposed to what it means to Offred.

Part X: Soul Scrolls

Chapter 25

Summary

Offred is awakened by a scream and a crash. Finding Offred asleep on the floor, half in the closet, Cora had thought her dead, a suicide, and in her shock has dropped the breakfast tray. If she brings a second breakfast, she will have to explain what happened, so Offred says she wasn't really hungry and will make do with the toast, still edible. Cora says she will pretend she dropped the tray and broke the dishes on the way out of Offred's room; Offred is pleased that Cora will lie for her.

Soon Offred visits the Commander two or three nights a week, whenever she is signalled by Nick. On the second visit, they again play Scrabble, then he offers her a treat: a glimpse at an old copy of *Vogue* magazine, something forbidden in Gilead.

She devours its fashion photos of bold, confident women, almost a different species from the women now. When Offred asks the Commander why he has it, he says that some in Gilead appreciate such things, which are not dangerous in the right hands.

At their third meeting, Offred asks him for some skin cream, and he brings her some at their next tryst. He is surprised when she says there is nowhere she can hide it because her room is searched. His ignorance angers her, but she uses the cream all the same.

Analysis

It is significant to Offred that Cora offers to lie about the broken dishes. Cora was always the friendlier of the two Marthas, but now she and Offred have a bond, a minor alliance.

The Commander's possession of a magazine (all of them were supposed to have been burned) is another sign that even those who wrote Gilead's laws can't live under them. His obvious elitism—claiming such things, while bad for the masses, are acceptable in his hands—loses him most of Offred's sympathy.

The chapter marks Offred's significant strengthening, if only she could see it. The Handmaid who, a short time ago, was friendless, powerless, and fearful of losing her sanity now has an ally in Cora and a degree of influence over the Commander.

Chapter 26

Summary

A month has passed and the Ceremony takes place again. Previously, Offred had been able to treat it as a distasteful duty to endure, but now she is troubled. When she sees the Commander that night, she feels awkward and shy. As she says, "He was no longer a thing to me."

She also feels differently about Serena Joy. Where once she experienced a pure and simple hatred for her, her feelings are now more complicated. She feels jealous of Serena Joy's connection to the Commander and guilty over her intrusion into the family, but she also is aware that she has a certain kind of power over her. This reminds her of Aunt Lydia's lecture on the future of women in Gilead: that they will live as one family, working for a common goal. The future, Aunt Lydia said, will hold greater freedom for generations of Handmaids. Each, for instance, will have a little garden.

Offred comes to an important conclusion about the Commander: she is no longer his sexual servant, but his mistress, and mistresses have clout. And she has a diversion, a way to pass those long, empty evenings. She is happier than she has been in a very long time. She realizes that she has become an individual to the Commander, just as he has to her.

Analysis

Offred's sense of power and new happiness have good and bad consequences. The good is that her life is much more bearable and she is not tempted by suicide. The bad is that, because she is happier, she may become complacent, less eager to escape and rejoin Luke, less willing to resist Gilead's domination.

Chapter 27

Summary

Shopping again with Ofglen, Offred notes that they are less suspicious of each other. Because of the heat of the June day, made more oppressive by their all-covering clothes, they take their time. They first pass the university, whose library, Offred thinks, is now empty of books. Then they pause at Soul Scrolls, one of Gilead's inventions. In this shop, Gilead's citizens can order computer-printed prayers, in person or by telephone. The five prayers are paid for by punching in one's computer number. Using the machines is a sign of religious devotion and loyalty to the state.

Offred realizes that Ofglen is looking at her—Offred—through the reflection in the store window. Then Ofglen comments, "Do you think God listens to these machines?" Despite her panic at this question, Offred manages to reply, "No." Suddenly they have crossed a fateful barrier. As they continue down the street, Ofglen murmurs, "You can join us."

On their return walk, they witness an arrest. Two Eyes swoop down on an ordinary man carrying a briefcase. He is bundled off into a black van and immediately driven away. All Offred feels is relief that she was not the one arrested.

Analysis

Soul Scrolls shows two things: the emptiness of Gilead's

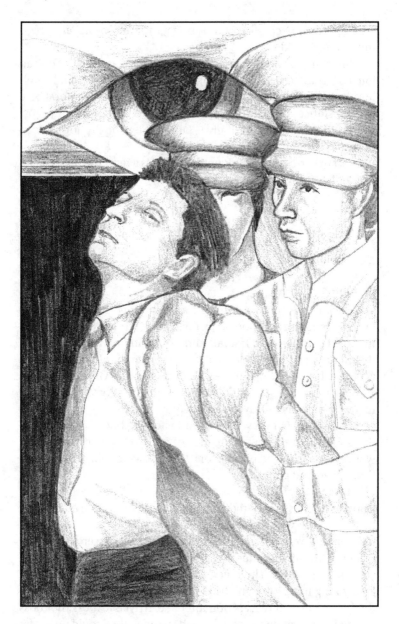

religion, now mechanized, and the fact that even prayer is regimented in Gilead.

Most important in this chapter is Ofglen's statement, "You can join us." This suggests something beyond Moira's individual rebellion and escape, or the grapevine of information and rumor. There is a resistance organization and Ofglen is part of it; it is not just something on television. It gives Offred a terrific lift, for she can become part of it.

But the arrest of the unidentified man is a reminder that Gilead is full of danger.

Chapter 28

Summary

Back in her room, Offred is too excited by Ofglen's words to take her required afternoon nap. Instead, she thinks of when Moira first declared herself a lesbian and of her affair with Luke before their marriage. She and Moira had argued over the affair, with Moira accusing her of hiding her head in the sand and Offred retorting, "If Moira thought she could create Utopia by shutting herself up in a woman-only enclave she was sadly mistaken."

Back then, Offred worked at transferring books to computer discs. She marvels now at the idea of millions of women going to work everyday and being paid for it. Like paper money, this is something dead and gone.

This prompts memories of Gilead's coup: the President and Congress were slaughtered and Islamic terrorists were blamed for it. Then there was "temporary" suspension of the Constitution, newspapers were censored and closed, roadblocks were set up, etc.

One morning on her way to work, she stopped at her usual store for cigarettes. The regular woman clerk had been replaced by a young man. When he tried her Compunumber on the register, it was rejected twice. Soon after she arrived at work, her boss entered in an agitated state, telling the women they could no longer work there—it was the law. Almost in tears, he apologized to them,

but insisted they leave, and Offred noticed two men armed with machine guns in the corridor. In a state of shock, the women filed out.

Back home, she had tried to telephone her mother, but there was no reply. She then tried Moira, who told her that all women's bank accounts had been frozen by the regime. Money, property, etc., would be transferred to their husbands, if they had them. Moira explained that the firings and the money freeze were put into effect suddenly and simultaneously to prevent people from fleeing the country.

Offred remembers trying to adapt to not being allowed to work or own property. And she remembers how Luke didn't think it was a travesty, and how Luke slid very easily into his role of breadwinner and caretaker of the family.

Analysis

Atwood's creation of a cashless society foreshadows a current movement toward the universal use of computerized money cards onto which the owner can load a certain amount of money. The card is then used instead of cash, even to buy newspapers or candy. But she shows that with such a system, whoever controls the computers controls the economy and society. The freedom of not having a pocketful of cash can be turned in a flash into a loss of the means to live.

Similarly, putting all books onto computer discs, then shredding the actual volumes, allows a regime to close down all access to information, or even to erase or alter it. And, as Gilead knows, knowledge is power. Atwood is saying that progress may come at a far steeper price than we are willing to pay, so we better not accept it blindly.

The banning of women from the workplace echoes what happened in Iran after its Islamic revolution, and what would later happen under Afghanistan's Taliban regime, which decreed that women not only could not hold jobs, they also were forbidden to go to school. All of this was done in the name of religion, for which many Islamic countries have condemned the Afghan regime.

Talking to Moira, Offred seems to feel regret and guilt that she has taken no active part in public affairs. Her timidity, like that of most Americans, has let the Gilead regime abandon constitutional government and rights with scarcely a shred of protest.

Thomas Jefferson wrote that the price of freedom is eternal vigilance, and Offred has learned the truth of that.

Chapter 29

Summary

Again, Offred plays Scrabble with the Commander. After he adds up their scores (Offred has won), he offers her a selection of reading material from Charles Dickens to copies of *Reader's Digest*. Offred says she would rather talk. She asks about him, and he tells her he once was in market research.

Next she asks him about the words scratched on her closet floor, but stumbles over their pronunciation. He pushes a pad and pen at her and tells her to write it down. It is the first time in years that she has been allowed to write, and it's awkward for her. She prints the words, *Nolite te bastardes carborundorum*, and passes the pad back to him.

He reads the message, then laughs. It is fake Latin, he tells her, the kind used by schoolboys. He takes down a Latin grammar book to show her some of the scribblings in its margins, including what she wrote. She asks what it means anyway, and he tells her: "Don't let the bastards grind you down."

Abruptly she asks, "What happened to her?" The Commander immediately knows who she means—the previous Handmaid, the one who left those words on the closet floor—and he tells Offred she hanged herself. Serena Joy found out about his secret meetings with her, he adds. He grows nervous that she will want to discontinue these meetings, and so he asks what she wants other than hand lotion. She replies that she wants to know "what's going on."

Analysis

The Commander's readiness to talk about the previous Handmaid's suicide can mean he is so confident that it doesn't matter what he tells Offred. Or it can mean that he finds his world so bleak and empty that he needs to talk. Offred seems to read it this second way: that despite the wall between them, they both are in the same prison, grasping at any chance of relief, however dangerous.

If this is true of this one important man, it is probably true throughout Gilead. Perhaps Gilead is beginning to crack from within. This, added to the war fronts and the sabotage campaigns, may mean that the end of Gilead is not all that far away.

Offred's question at the end of the chapter—"What's going on?"—asks about the whole direction in which Gilead is heading, not just what is happening between the Commander and her. It is the ultimate question.

SECTION TWELVE

Part XI: Night

Chapter 30

Summary

In bed, Offred lets her thoughts drift to the past. She remembers the attempt she and Luke made to escape to Canada after she was fired from her job, when the shape of Gilead became obvious. They tried to make it look like they were just going for a picnic in the country, so their home had to look normal, and they could scarcely take anything with them.

The one problem was the family cat: they couldn't take it, nor could leave it, for it might yowl after a day or two and give away their escape. Luke takes on the wretched job of killing the cat, and Offred sees this as a cost of dictatorship: "They force you to kill...."

She tries to visualize Luke and her daughter, and is upset that their faces won't come into focus. She can't bear to lose those memories.

She remembers the prayers they had to say at the Center, kneeling on the wooden floor: "Oh God, King of the universe, thank you for not creating me a man. Oh God, obliterate me. Make me fruitful. Mortify my flesh, that I may be multiplied. Let me be fulfilled..."

She thinks now of God, wondering what He can be up to. Is He fed up? She would be. She wishes God would speak to her in her loneliness.

Analysis

Since Offred is a Handmaid, we know her escape attempt failed. But we can wonder how many others attempted escape and what happened to them. Perhaps some did make it to freedom. Probably many died in the attempt. And the rest, like Offred, were captured and regimented by the state.

The prayer she and the other Handmaid-trainees recited is an amplification of what Offred ruefully said to her absent mother earlier: "You wanted a women's culture."

Study Questions

1. Why does Cora panic when she sees Offred asleep on the floor?

2. What is important about the models in the copy of *Vogue*?

3. How does the Commander justify having copies of fashion magazines such as *Vogue* if they were supposed to have been burned during the revolution?

4. How does Offred feel power over Serena Joy?

5. Why is Offred so hesitant to reply to Ofglen's question about the Soul Scrolls?

6. What do the Soul Scrolls reveal about the spirituality of Gilead?

7. How was Gilead able to kill the President and Congress?

8. During the revolution, why did the government freeze women's bank accounts at the same time that it dismissed women from their jobs?

9. What does Offred realize when the Commander shows her that *Nolite te bastardes carborundorum* came from the margins of his textbook?

10. What is the significance of the Handmaids' prayer at the Red Center?

Answers

1. Offred has wondered about her predecessor a great deal,

even imagining her manner and looks. This woman hanged herself, apparently in this same room. Cora may have been the first one to find the body. So, finding Offred, still dressed in her gown and lying halfway in the closet, she must have thought this was another suicide.

2. Handmaids are conditioned to modesty, walking with bowed heads, avoiding other people's eyes. But the models in *Vogue* seem proud and defiant, some standing with their feet apart like buccaneers. They wear a great variety of clothes of many colors and materials, unlike Handmaids who wear a single uniform, so the models virtually shout, "We have choice!"

3. The Commander argues that these outlawed materials would be dangerous in the hands of the masses but harmless for those in power. One sign of a totalitarian government is that the leaders tend to exempt themselves from the rules established for the society and to generally mistrust those without power.

4. The Commander, in these secret evening trysts, is clearly more casual with Offred than he ever appears to be with Serena Joy. He is also probably more open to requests from Offred than he is from his wife. If Serena Joy knew this, she would be humiliated that a servant has a greater effect on her husband than she does. Offred enjoys this feeling of power over her rival, even though Serena Joy is unaware of it.

5. Even before the episode of the arrest of the man with the briefcase, Offred has reason to be cautious—even paranoid—about expressing herself to others. Gilead is full of spies and informers, so Ofglen's cynical comment on the Soul Scrolls may be a trap for her. All the same, she has begun to feel a rapport with Ofglen, so her shy "No" is a small step toward establishing trust.

6. The Soul Scrolls indicate that while Gileadean society is structured almost entirely on biblical concepts, it is spiritually bankrupt. Prayers for health, wealth, death, birth, and sins can be purchased—reminiscent of the corrupt system

of selling indulgences in the Middle Ages—and then recited not by a person but by a machine. These gestures are clearly intended as signs of true piety and faithfulness to the regime rather than to God.

7. The Commander was in market research, he says, before the revolution. Other leaders of the revolution must have been similarly substantial citizens. They would have had access to members of Congress, even the President, as leaders of business and their communities. They were insiders, which gave them opportunities that most others would have been denied. Change—even revolution—is far easier to accomplish from inside than from outside.

8. Women's bank accounts were frozen at the same time that women lost their jobs so that they would not have the resources to flee the country. The regime especially did not want to lose women such as Offred since they represented the greatest national treasure—potential reproductivity.

9. Seeing the Latin phrase in the Commander's textbook, Offred realizes that her predecessor also made these illegal visits to the Commander's study. When the Commander goes on to tell Offred that the previous Offred committed suicide because Serena Joy found out about their trysts, she sees that he is equally willing to put her in as dangerous a position.

10. The prayer is meant to be self-abasing, a statement that women's only purpose is to bear children. Praying to be "fulfilled" is ironic, because we never see a single Handmaid who seems fulfilled.

Suggested Essay Topics

1. Discuss ways in which Gilead demonstrates that it is a patriarchal misogynic society, and its justification for this.

2. How is the treatment of Handmaids similar to that of Jews in Nazi Germany, inside and outside the concentration camps?

3. In Gilead, a woman's body entirely determines her role in society. Discuss the ways this is, and is not, true in today's society.

Part XII: Jezebel's

Chapter 31

Summary

It is July fifth, and Offred now has a lighter-weight version of the Handmaid gown. On another shopping trip she and Ofglen find two new corpses hung on the Wall, one a Catholic wearing a placard with an upside-down cross, the other marked with the letter J. Since Jewish corpses bear a yellow star, Offred wonders what this J stands for: Jehovah's Witness, perhaps, or Jesuit. All religions except Gilead's official one are banned.

They pass what once was Memorial Hall, where undergraduates ate in the early days of the university. Moira had told her that women were forbidden to enter; if they did, they were pelted with buns. She doesn't like Moira's holding a grudge over something that happened in the past.

Pausing there, Ofglen tells Offred what "us" means: it refers to Mayday, the underground network. She says it is highly compartmentalized, so if anyone is interrogated, she will know only a few other members.

Back home, Offred sees Nick's signal that the Commander wants to see her that night. On her way to the back door, Offred is called over by Serena Joy, who says she can sit and offers her a cushion. Serena Joy asks if there is any sign yet of pregnancy and, when Offred says no, remarks, "Your time is running out." She adds:

"Maybe he can't.... Maybe you should try it another way." She adds that Ofwarren was made pregnant by a doctor, and suggests Offred try this, but with Nick.

Offred agrees, and Serena Joy promises her a bribe: a current picture of her daughter. She gives Offred a cigarette and tells her to get a match from the Marthas.

Analysis

Serena Joy's comment, "Your time is running out," could mean Offred's term at this posting is nearly done and she'll be reposted. But more likely it seems she has little time left as a Handmaid, since this is her third posting. So her life is running out.

Serena Joy's suggestion that the Commander can't father a child and that Offred will have to look elsewhere is a real shock. It's forbidden in Gilead to suggest that a man can't produce viable sperm. In Gilead, only women are infertile; if there is no child, it is the woman's fault. Serena's suggestion is treasonous.

That she knows how Ofwarren got pregnant suggests there is a Wives' conspiracy to break Gilead's laws. How could she know this unless the other Wife told her?

Her suggestion that Offred allow Nick to impregnate her, thus making her a co-conspirator to adultery, shows how far she is willing to go to get what she wants.

Perhaps Serena Joy, with only her gardening and scarf-knitting, is so desperate for a child to fill the void in her life that she is sincere in what she proposes. Yet, Offred knows how deeply Serena Joy dislikes her, so she must suspect that this is a trap with fatal consequences. Yet, bearing a child is her only means of staying alive, so that she eventually can escape Gilead and be reunited with Luke and her daughter.

The cigarette bribe is nothing compared to the offer of a photograph of her daughter as she is today, a bribe impossible to resist.

Chapter 32

Summary

As Serena Joy told her, Offred asks Rita for a match. After much persuading, an irritated Rita gets one from the locked cupboard and warns Offred not to set fire to her room. Then she pops an ice cube in her mouth and offers one to Offred, her first act of kindness.

Upstairs, Offred doesn't know what to do. She would enjoy the cigarette, but enjoys owning the match even more. As Rita said, it could start a fire and burn the house down.

She thinks about having spent the last evening with the Commander, who has begun to drink in her presence. Sometimes, when a little drunk, he plays Radio Free America's uncensored news for a few minutes. Ofglen has told her he is one of the regime's top men but, alone with him, Offred finds this hard to believe.

He is increasingly open with her, telling her, for instance, that one of the reasons for Gilead was that women had become just too easily available, so men were turned off, thus causing the birthrate to fall. "We thought we could do better," he says, and there is a hint that he realizes they have failed to do so.

Later, in bed, Offred looks at the ceiling's circle of plaster flowers, where a chandelier used to be, the chandelier from which the previous Offred hung herself.

Analysis

Offred probably knows the match is not power, merely the illusion of it. It could fail, or whatever she tried to set on fire might not burn. But the illusion is better than nothing.

The Commander's drinking and wistfulness are further evidence that Gilead may be crumbling at the top. Of course, this does not mean that the leadership can admit its mistakes and allow the former America to be restored. Too many people would want vengeance. The leaders would be tried, imprisoned, perhaps executed. They are on a wild horse they dare not try to get off, but their pleasure in the ride has clearly vanished.

Chapter 33

Summary

One July afternoon, Offred and Ofglen are summoned to a women's Prayvaganza in a courtyard of the university, passing through a checkpoint manned by armed Guardians. A section of the courtyard has been roped off for Handmaids, and chairs are set out for Wives. Ofglen urges Offred to head for the back, where there will be a better chance to talk. As they kneel, they notice Ofwarren enter the courtyard.

Offred wonders why Ofwarren is there so soon after her delivery. But Ofglen informs her the baby was a shredder after all, the second one Ofwarren has had, significantly increasing her chances of being sent to the Colonies. Ofwarren looks thin and dazed as she kneels with the others.

Offred remembers when she and Moira saw Ofwarren at the Red Center, round-eyed and with a grimace of a smile, saying to no one, "My name's Janine. I'm your waitperson for this morning. Can I get you some coffee to begin with?" Moira had slapped her hard, and Janine had returned to reality. Had she fallen into insanity, she would have been killed. It looks now as if Ofwarren is again close to the breaking point.

Analysis

Gilead is by no means the first society to have special women's religious festivals. Among others, the Greeks and Romans had women's temples and goddesses, and the men had theirs. The temples of Aphrodite, Vesta, and others were forbidden to men, and the penalties for trespassing were severe. The rationale was that men and women had different needs; therefore, they had their special gods and goddesses to attend to those needs.

But Gilead segregates the sexes and its social classes not to suit their needs, but to maintain control. The fear and jealousy the different groups feel toward each other prevents the creation of alliances that might threaten the regime.

That Ofwarren is in danger of exile is frightening, since no

Handmaid has been so subservient to the Aunts as she has, and she has done her best to be a good Handmaid. Such loyalty to Gilead really counts for nothing in the long run, if healthy children are not produced.

Chapter 34

Summary

Still at the Prayvaganza, Offred watches a Commander open the proceedings, then they sing the old hymn, "There Is a Balm in Gilead." Offred remembers Moira's version: "There Is a Bomb in Gilead." Next, 20 Angels, newly returned from the front, enter for their marriage ceremony. They are joined by 20 veiled young women in white with their mothers. These marriages have been arranged by the authorities.

Offred remembers her discussion of what is missing in Gilead. When she asks him about love, he replies that arranged marriages work out better. Now, with arranged marriages, nobody is left out, the Commander has told her.

The couples kneel and the Commander leads them through their vows, which remind the brides of their secondary place as servants to their husbands, and the ceremony is done.

As they leave, Ofglen tells Offred that "we" (Mayday) know of her evenings with the Commander, and asks Offred what happens. Offred answers ambiguously. Before parting, Ofglen tells her to find out anything she can from the Commander, anything at all about Gilead.

Analysis

As mentioned in the analysis of Chapter 3, the biblical Gilead was the land east of the Jordan River, home of the state of Jordan today. It was famous for the wound-healing balm made from the sap of its trees. The hymn speaks of a metaphorical balm: "There is a balm in Gilead to heal the sin-sick soul."

But there is nothing soothing, restful, and uplifting in the Republic of Gilead. So Moira's "There Is a Bomb in Gilead" is true; in fact, Gilead is a country full of bombs—time bombs—just waiting to explode in revolution. Now, with Mayday, these bombs are combining their explosive force.

Chapter 35

Summary

Offred recalls her escape attempt with Luke and the false passports they carried because Gilead had nullified all divorces, and Luke had been married before. At the border, Luke panicked when a guard went inside to check out the passports. He reversed the car and sped down a dirt road into the woods. When the road ended, he, Offred, and their daughter raced for Canada.

Abruptly, she returns to her conversation with the Commander, their talk about love. "Falling" in love, she thinks, is a free fall, easy but scary. She thinks of the frightening side of sex: attack, rape, fear of walking along streets at night, all things Gilead has eliminated. Things should feel better, but they don't.

She weeps at the emptiness of her life, but is interrupted by a knock at the door. It is Serena Joy, and she has brought the picture of Offred's daughter. She is tall, dressed in white, changed, showing what the past three years have done to her. Offred realizes that she must be just a dim shadow in her daughter's mind. So, although she is relieved to see that her daughter is alive and well, she feels tremendous grief, too. Offred wishes she had not seen the picture.

As she sits down to her lunch of creamed corn and diced meat, equipped with only a fork and spoon, she longs for a knife.

Analysis

Gilead's elimination of divorce, even those that took place before the revolution, is one more elimination of choice. The same is true of its arranged marriages: total strangers linked for life. But since Gilead is concerned about population growth, not human happiness, these marriages are appropriate.

Given that Luke and Offred were heading from the Boston area, they would have gone through Vermont to Québec, or through Maine to New Brunswick. Either way, the forests have many logging roads they could have used, just as bootleggers did during Prohibition in the 1920s. They probably would have been wiser to use them instead of trying to brazen it out on a main highway. They would have had a better chance.

Offred's misery after seeing her daughter's picture and her longing to get hold of a knife are bad signs. It seems likely she wants the knife for a suicide attempt rather than to help her escape. Her increasing sense of empowerment seems to have been destroyed by the photograph.

Chapter 36

Summary

At Offred's next visit to the Commander, he greets her with the words, "How is the fair little one this evening?" He has a surprise for her, but she must try to guess what it is. When she can't, he holds out to her a pink and mauve showgirl outfit with sequined bodice and feathers. She remembers news clips of such things being destroyed in Gilead's early days. He tells her to put it on and to "paint your face too."

He turns his back while she strips off her Handmaid rig and dons this skimpy, tacky outfit and the high-heeled shoes that go with it, as ill-fitting as the costume. The make-up he offers is cheap lipstick and mascara. She is so unused to it that she makes a mess and must redo it.

They drive off in his Whirlwind. At one point the Commander tells her to get down on the floor. They pass through a checkpoint, then drive on to their destination. Offred desperately wants a mirror, to see if her lipstick is on straight.

Analysis

The Commander's coyness makes him seem like a teenager rather than one of the powers of Gilead. That he's had several drinks suggests he is trying to add some zest to his life.

The costume he gives Offred is just another indication of his readiness to flout Gilead's rules. It is a costume intended to turn a woman into a sex object.

Offred knows that the Commander's proposal is extremely risky for her, but apparently she is just as anxious as he is to enjoy a real break from the dullness of her life.

Chapter 37

Summary

Passing through two doors, Offred and the Commander enter a softly lit, carpeted hallway lined with numbered doors, apparently a former hotel. Beyond is a central atrium, several stories high, capped with a vast skylight. Its fountain, glass-walled elevators, and vine-hung balconies remind Offred that she was here once with Luke.

Many older men, some in Commander's uniforms, are seated on the chairs and sofas: these are the movers and shakers of Gilead. But the women are the real surprise. All are dressed scantily in short nightgowns, bathing suits, old cheerleader uniforms, etc. "It's like walking into the past," says the Commander, but Offred thinks it's more like some sad children's masquerade party.

He takes her around the room to show her off, then seats her on a sofa. She asks what all this means and he says, "It means you can't cheat Nature. Nature demands variety, for men." Then he points out certain women: one used to be a sociologist, another a lawyer, a third a business executive. Now they are prostitutes, but amusing to talk to. He offers to get Offred a drink; she asks for a weak gin and tonic.

When he leaves, Offred suffers her biggest shock: she sees Moira by the fountain, clad in a Playboy bunny outfit, its ears bedraggled. Moira here? Then Moira sees her, too. They stare at each other, then Moira gives her their Red Center signal that means they must meet in the washroom.

When the Commander returns with the drinks, Offred asks

where the washroom is. Walking awkwardly in her new high heels, she heads for her secret meeting with Moira.

Analysis

Jezebel's is named for the wife of the biblical King Ahab, who seduced her husband into abandoning Jehovah. When Ahab was overthrown for this, she was killed, and her body thrown into the street and eaten by dogs. This secret nightclub for Gilead's elite is named in her honor, which is symbolic.

Offred's spotting of Moira shocks Offred and the reader. Moira was supposed to have made it to freedom. Offred needed to believe that because it gave her hope for herself. But if a bold, inventive person like Moira can't get free, what chance is there for her?

And why is Moira here? She was a strident feminist, with contempt for men, and a lesbian. That she should be working as a prostitute for Gilead's elite males, wearing a worn-out bunny costume, is utterly perverse. Has she surrendered? Is there no way out of Gilead?

Chapter 38

Summary

Inside the washroom Offred finds a huge mirror of real glass. The two rooms are still their original pink, including the sinks. Several women sit on the sofa and chairs, with their shoes off, smoking and unsmiling. Then Moira emerges from a toilet cubicle. They kiss, then look each other over in their ridiculous costumes. They sit down and Moira asks Offred what has brought her here to Jezebel's.

Moira tells what happened to her after she strode out of the Red Center, leaving Aunt Elizabeth "tied up like a Christmas turkey." She had walked through town, head high, shoulders back, as if she were on a duty mission. She went to an address she remembered from the women's collective days, people who had a Q beside their names, for Quaker. This proved successful, and she was

taken in, fed, and passed on to another Quaker home, part of the Underground Femaleroad spiriting fugitive women out of the country. It was very well organized, she assures Offred. This, she says, was while Gilead was going after Jews, African Americans, and other minorities, but before it began arresting members of other Christian denominations.

She was taken as far as Maine, but someone must have snitched. As she was coming out of the house where she was hidden to begin the last leg of her journey, she and the couple hiding her were arrested.

After her arrest Moira was shown a film of women's life in the Colonies, cleaning up toxic waste and burning bodies after battles. Three years, Moira tells Offred, is the longest one can stay alive in the Colonies. Most of the women are older, some very old, which is why there are so few of them on the streets anymore.

Moira was shown the film to pressure her: either she became a state prostitute or she would be shipped to some Colony as a slave and die. "I'm not a martyr," she explains.

Offred cannot accept this. She needed to believe that people like Moira would never surrender, that Moira would die rather than give in.

Moira refers to Jezebel's as "butch paradise," since none of the women there like men. This meeting in the bathroom is the last time Offred ever sees Moira.

She adds that she would like to think that Moira escaped again, or blew up Jezebel's, killing 50 Commanders. But she knows this isn't true.

Analysis

Moira's good words about the Underground Femaleroad are more than offset by the fact that she was caught while using it. It may be organized, but it isn't safe. Vastly more daunting to Offred, though, is the fact that Moira has settled for life at Jezebel's, which is only a brief reprieve before exile and death. Offred's role model has given up.

That the Underground Femaleroad is largely Quaker-run echoes the Underground Railroad that smuggled slaves out of the South through the northern states and into Canada. Great

numbers of Quaker volunteers operated the Underground Railroad at considerable risk.

The Quaker movement, (or, to give it its official name, the Society of Friends) began with George Fox, a shoemaker in Nottingham, England, who broke with the formalism of the Church of England in 1646. He stressed divine inspiration—"the inner light"—rather than dogma. The movement's beliefs include active humanitarianism and renunciation of violence. Their belief in human equality made them ardent abolitionists and gave them a key role in the Underground Railroad.

Chapter 39

Summary

When Offred returns from the washroom, the Commander takes her to one of the private rooms. Offred hides in the bathroom, washing her face and savoring the smell of good soap, then sits on the bathtub's side, unwilling to return to the Commander.

Moira told her that her mother was sent to the Colonies; Moira recognized her in the film she was shown. Offred remembers trying to telephone her mother when things began to get oppressive in Gilead. When she repeatedly got no answer, she drove with Luke to her mother's apartment building. Her mother's apartment was in chaos: the mattress was cut open, the bureau drawers were dumped. Offred had wanted to call the police, but Luke hadn't let her. She could find no trace of her mother.

She remembers that at college, Moira had called her mother "neat," which had surprised Offred. Now she thinks of her mother cleaning up deadly spills in the Colonies.

Finally she emerges from the bathroom to find the Commander lying on the king-size bed, his shoes off. Offred thinks that if she must have sex with him, she would rather it be at the impersonal Ceremony. When he reaches for her, she feels rage, contempt, and even pity—but she cannot respond to him.

Analysis

While the Commander waits on the king-size bed in lustful anticipation, Offred sits in the bathroom, mourning her mother but unable to tell him so. This shows that this is no real relationship, not even a kind of friendship, just an empty arrangement of strangers.

Moira has told Offred, in effect, that her mother is dead, since exiles in the Colonies have three years of life at most. It is more than three years since Offred's mother disappeared (when she disappeared, Offred obviously had not yet made her escape attempt, and that was more than three years ago). So her mother can't still be alive.

For all that they disagreed, Offred loved her mother, and should have a right to mourn her properly, rather than being locked in a bathroom with her memories for a few minutes while a randy stranger waits in the next room to take her to bed.

Part XIII: Night

Chapter 40

Summary

Having returned from Jezebel's, Offred waits, dressed, on her bed. At midnight there is a soft tapping at her door. It is Serena Joy. She leads Offred downstairs to the back door. Offred makes her way outside to the door that leads to Nick's apartment over the garage.

Offred offers two different versions of her encounter with Nick. In the first version, they immediately make passionate love. In the second version, she climbs the stairs and knocks at the apartment door. Nick lets her in and offers her his cigarette. They stand looking at each other awkwardly. Then Offred says, "I know it's hard for you." Nick responds, "I get paid." The tension is broken when each of them throws out a corny old pickup line. Soon after—for it is extremely dangerous for her to be here—they make love on Nick's spartan bed.

Afterwards, Offred feels guilty about her unfaithfulness to Luke, who may still be alive, and about being so sexually responsive to Nick.

Analysis

Offred doesn't explain how Serena Joy has negotiated Offred's tryst with Nick, or does she repeat reassurances Serena Joy may have made. So from Offred's point of view, this may be like stepping into a minefield. All Serena Joy has to do is pick up the telephone, call the Eyes, have them break into Nick's apartment, and Nick and Offred are doomed. Apparently, though, her desire for a baby is stronger than her other feelings, so the two are safe.

Offred and Nick's meeting is like a blind date, full of awkwardness. But their mutual need overcomes this. It is the first time in years that Offred has been held by someone she doesn't pity or hate, and being held is something she can scarcely exist without. For a brief time she can erase Gilead, Moira, her mother, and the fate of her husband and daughter, even her own potential fate. It's worth the risk.

And if she does become pregnant by Nick, she no longer will be living on borrowed time, facing the same fate as her mother.

Study Questions

1. What bothers Offred about Moira's recollection that women once were banned from Memorial Hall?

2. Is there any truth to the Commander's idea that men were turned off by sex in pre-Gilead America because of women's availability?

3. What does the Commander's statement "You can't make an omelette without breaking eggs" mean?

4. What is Ofwarren's/Janine's role in the novel?

5. Is Offred a wimp, as Moira suggests?

6. How does Offred know that the Commander has taken such an adventure before?

7. What is the significance of the fact that a number of the prostitutes at Jezebel's were professional women in the days before the revolution?

8. Moira worried that the Quaker family would not open the door to her because she was dressed in an Aunt's outfit. Why is it significant that this did not happen?

9. Why does Moira lose her will to resist?

10. Why does Luke resist Offred's suggestion to call the police after her mother's disappearance?

Answers

1. Moira's raking up past affronts to women bothers Offred because she does not share Moira's grievance against men and because it only helps preserve those old divisions. There comes a time, she suggests, when you have to leave the past behind and live in the present. The implications of this disagreement are vast. For example, should African Americans demand compensation because their ancestors were stolen out of Africa, shipped across the Atlantic, and enslaved for generations? Should Jews hold present-day Germany liable for the Holocaust? Thousands of such grievances can be made against past injustices. Is there a historical statute of limitations that decrees when past crimes must be treated as over and done?

2. The Commander blames women's sexual availability for the falling birthrate. This seems unrealistic—part of Gilead's policy of blaming women for most failures.

3. The Commander's "breaking eggs to make an omelette" statement comes from Lenin, founder of the Soviet Union. He inaugurated a policy of terror in 1919 that led directly to the Stalinist terror of the 1930s which killed perhaps as many as 30 million people, far more than Hitler's genocide. It is a facile phrase and obscures the fact that it is not eggs that are being broken, but human beings. In effect, the Commander is glibly rationalizing the murder of thousands—even millions—of people and the ruination of the lives of millions more to achieve Gilead's goals. It ties him to all of history's murderous dictators.

4. Janine clearly is put into the novel to show the debilitating effects of Gilead on a woman who lacks any real strength: it sends her over the brink into madness. She also shows that it is almost impossible for a Handmaid to win in Gilead. She ingratiated herself with the Aunts at the Red Center and has

become pregnant twice as a Handmaid, so she has done all the right things. Still she is doomed.

5. Offred is nothing like what Janine is. In fact, Offred stands midway between the two extremes of Janine (total slave to Gilead) and Moira (total rebel). She is a sort of Everywoman, representing the majority of women who have a clear sense of self, who achieve an education and a job, but who are not strident.

6. The Commander's instructions to Nick suggest that this adventure is routine for him. In addition, he has a key to the door of the establishment. The outfit that he provides Offred has been worn before, perhaps by the previous Offred.

7. These women—including the sociologist, the lawyer, and the business executive—have opted to become prostitutes rather than Handmaids or Marthas because they can retain some degree of free expression. That the men appreciate the conversation these women can offer suggests that it is not just the sex that attracts them to the club.

8. The Quaker family was not alarmed by Moira's appearance because the Aunts and even the Center were hardly common knowledge in the early days of the regime. As with the extermination of Jews in the concentration camps, the mental and physical abuse of the Handmaids was kept secret at first. By the time people were aware of the policies that made up this reproduction program, it was too dangerous to raise objections or to form a protest.

9. Like Offred, Moira was given the choice to do what was asked of her or to go to the Colonies. After viewing the film about the Colonies, she knows there really is no choice involved. Her work as a prostitute at least allows her relative safety and some freedom of expression in the company of the other prostitutes, although she will lose even these liberties in a few years.

10. Luke realizes it is likely that it was the police who ransacked his mother-in-law's apartment and abducted her. Since Offred's mother was an ardent feminist and activist in the

pre-Gilead days, the government probably considered her a threat that needed to be silenced.

Suggested Essay Topics

1. Discuss the use of computers for good and ill in Gilead.

2. "There Is a Balm in Gilead" was a well-known Negro spiritual. Explore this link as well as the many other connections between Gilead and antebellum America that Atwood is establishing in this novel.

3. Protestantism is based on an individual's relationship with God, with no intermediaries. Show how Soul Scrolls and other aspects of "Protestant" Gilead deny that personal relationship.

Part XIV: Salvaging

Chapter 41

Summary

Offred apologizes for her story's fragmentary nature, its pain, and lack of resolution. She says how hard it is having to relive these events and suffer her devastating boredom, but she is determined to hide nothing. She is even determined to honestly relate the part of her story in which she claims she does not behave well.

She says she chooses to return to Nick's room on many evenings. Although their affair is very dangerous, she still views his apartment as a haven of safety "where we huddle together while the storm goes on outside." She tells him her real name and confides in him about everything except Luke and the previous Offred. Nick tells her little about himself.

One night, she has Nick put his hand on her belly to feel the new life stirring inside her—but she's not sure it's true. Perhaps it's just wishful thinking, as it is too early to tell.

Ofglen encourages Offred to go into her Commander's study to look through his papers, but Offred shies away from this, saying she is afraid. In actuality, she has grown indifferent to the Commander, now that she has become so serious about Nick. When Ofglen pressures her again to work for the resistance, promising her that the Mayday people could get her out if it became too dangerous, Offred realizes she no longer even desires escape. "I want to be here with Nick, where I can get at him," she says to herself. Ofglen senses her apathy and starts to give up on her.

Analysis

So much of the novel has dealt with Offred's misery at the Commander's house, her desire to escape and rejoin her husband and daughter, and her temptation to follow her predecessor's example by killing herself that the reader may be surprised that she doesn't jump at the chance for freedom.

But this is very human. Someone freed after a long prison term frequently finds the outside world terrifying. There are so many choices, and the imprisoned have lost the ability to make choices after years of being told when to wake, eat, shower, and so on.

In addition, and perhaps more importantly, Offred has developed serious feelings for Nick, and this results in her sense of complacency. She loses interest in both the resistance movement and her own escape as the sinks deeper into the illusion that she can build a life with Nick in these circumstances. By suggesting this change in Offred's character, Atwood is perhaps illustrating the dangers that can result when women allow men and their romantic ties to these men to become their sole focus. This type of complacency may have helped enable the leaders of Gilead to stage their revolution with relative ease.

Chapter 42

Summary

While a bell tolls in the background, Ofglen and Offred head for the university. At the main gate a large group of Angels in riot gear stands by. There is to be a Salvaging for women only.

A wooden stage has been erected in front of the former library that reminds Offred of the graduation ceremonies of the past. She remarks that this is her second Salvaging. Wives and their daughters are seated on folding chairs at the back, then Marthas and Econowives, and Handmaids kneel in the front on velvet cushions.

The three who are to be salvaged are seated on the stage. A procession enters: Aunt Lydia of the Red Center and two black-hooded Salvagers. Aunt Lydia speaks to the crowd for several minutes, then takes a paper from her pocket and calls out the name of the first of the three who will be salvaged.

Offred has seen this before—the victim stands on a stool, the white bag is placed over her head and a noose around her neck, then the stool is kicked away, there is a death struggle, and finally the body goes limp. She cannot look, so she stares at the grass.

But, there is a difference in this Salvaging. Previously, the victim's crimes had been read out before the execution. This time they were not.

Analysis

That Gilead's executions are sexually segregated is part of Gilead's perverse "women's culture." Only women hang women.

The victims' crimes are no longer announced because the authorities don't want others to know what the crimes are because they might imitate them.

The term *Salvaging* combines "salvation" and "savaging" and sums up Gilead beautifully: savagery masquerading as holiness.

Gilead's public executions are another return to the past. A few countries, mostly dictatorships, still hold public executions. But most did away with them years, even centuries, ago. When he was very young, Charles Dickens saw one in London, one of the last there. Almost all Western countries have done away with all forms of execution within the last 25 years. The most notable exception is the United States.

One of the primary reasons for public, or any other, executions is that they provide a cautionary lesson to others, those who otherwise might commit crimes. Of course, there is evidence to the contrary. The abandonment of executions is inevitably followed by a decline in the crime rate, not a rise.

All Gilead is doing is exercising its blood lust.

Chapter 43

Summary

The three victims, with the white sacks over their heads, remind Offred of chickens hanging in a poultry shop window. The Salvaging is over.

Now comes the Particicution. Aunt Lydia cautions the Handmaids to wait for her whistle, and two Guardians lead in a third Guardian. He can scarcely walk and his face is battered and swollen. Aunt Lydia says he has been convicted of rape, and the penalty is meted out according to Deuteronomy. A collective sigh comes from the women, and Offred says she can feel the blood lust rising in her.

Aunt Lydia smiles, then blows her whistle. The convicted man is freed: he staggers and almost falls. The Handmaids pause, then surge forward, punching, kicking, and screaming. Offred sees Ofglen push the victim down and kick him hard three times in the head. Then she retreats as the other Handmaids finish him off.

Offred is shocked at Ofglen's brutality, but Ofglen curtly tells her the man wasn't a rapist. He was a member of Mayday. She kicked him so hard to stun him, to put him beyond pain.

Again, Aunt Lydia blows her whistle and the two Guardians carry off the body. Janine wanders past Offred, blood smeared on her cheek, her eyes glassy, giggling. "You have a nice day," she says as she passes. For a moment Offred envies Janine's lapse into madness.

Back at home, even though she took no part in the killing, Offred fiercely scrubs her hands to wash away the smell of tar.

Analysis

Atwood clearly has taken the title for the second part of this ceremony from a Canadian government fitness program, Participaction, begun in 1972.

Although Aunt Lydia's justifications for this murderous brutality is that it's from the Bible, the actual Deuteronomy text reads, "But if a man find a betrothed damsel in the field, and the man

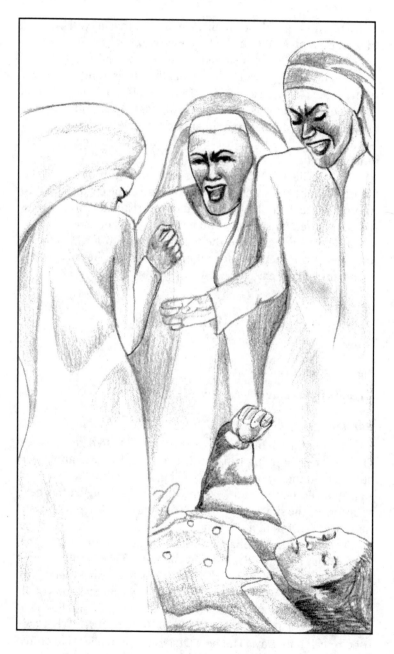

force her, and lie with her, then the man only that lay with her shall die." It then prescribes death by public stoning.

But this man is not stoned to death; he is punched, kicked, scratched, perhaps even bitten to death. This is hands-on execution, as the blood on Janine's face shows. It is much like the ritual orgies of the Maenads, female worshippers of the god Dionysus. These women, dressed in animal skins, danced and drank themselves into a frenzy, then tore apart any animal or man they encountered.

This is Gilead's "ecumenical" side again: a mix of Marxist slogans, Milton's poetry, and biblical texts, with some pagan bloodlust, murderous racism, and fundamentalist Christianity thrown in. No wonder Offred must scrub until her hands are almost raw.

If Ofglen is right, and the victim was killed for his Mayday membership rather than for rape, this clearly is because Gilead wants to hide the existence of Mayday.

Chapter 44

New Character:

Ofglen's replacement: *also named Ofglen*

Summary

After her usual bland, but healthy lunch, Offred goes to meet Ofglen for a shopping trip. But it is not Ofglen who appears. A stranger, thinner and paler than Ofglen, greets Offred with the formal "Blessed be the fruit." When Offred asks if Ofglen has been transferred, the stranger answers, "I am Ofglen." Offred wishes she had asked her friend her real name.

They pass three female corpses on the Wall, the women executed that morning. Offred and the new Ofglen walk by them wordlessly. On the way home, Offred says of her former friend, "I've known her since May," a cue to see if the new woman knows of the Mayday network. Offred flushes when she says this and her heart races. She adds that it was at the beginning of May, "What they used to call May Day." The new Ofglen coldly replies that Offred should forget such vestiges of the past. Offred concludes this new-comer is not one of "us," but she is aware of Mayday, and apparently is trying to warn Offred to give up thoughts of resistance.

Offred is frightened and thinks of all the ways she can be tortured. They can threaten to harm her daughter; if Luke is alive and a prisoner, they can harm him. They can make her confess, make her testify against the other Ofglen, make her tell everything she knows about Mayday.

Then, just before leaving, the new Ofglen whispers, "She hanged herself." Ofglen had seen an Eyes' van coming for her, this woman explains. "It was better," she says, and walks off.

Analysis

The first Ofglen's near-arrest and suicide, like that morning's killing festival, shows Gilead's brutality as well as Mayday's vulnerability. Perhaps Offred was right to not accept Ofglen's offer of escape. Better safe than sorry. Except, of course, she isn't safe at all unless she becomes pregnant.

Chapter 45

Summary

Learning of Ofglen's suicide makes Offred feel she's had the air kicked out of her. She doesn't want to die or to be one of those creatures strung up on the Wall. She will do anything to stay alive. She feels overwhelmed by Gilead's power.

She heads for the house's back door, only to be confronted in the garden by Serena Joy, who has found out about her secret meetings with the Commander and their trip to Jezebel's. She flings down the sequined, feathered showgirl costume. "Behind my back," she accuses. "Just like the other one. A slut."

Offred picks up the costume and goes to her room.

Analysis

Serena Joy's confrontation takes away what little ground Offred still has under her feet. Before, Serena Joy was willing to conspire with her about Nick, despite her dislike of Offred. Now she has become an outraged enemy, one with resources.

Offred's new willingness to abase herself to Gilead is now impossible. She cannot stay in this house, and probably can't stay alive in Gilead, but she has no way now of contacting Mayday. Only death awaits her; her only choice is whether it be by Salvaging or suicide.

Part XV: Night

Chapter 46

Summary

That night Offred waits in her room. Soon they will be coming to arrest her. Yet, she feels "serene, at peace...." She repeats the phrase scratched on her closet floor— "Don't let the bastards grind you down"—like a mantra.

She still has the match, she reminds herself. Setting the house ablaze, she could take her death into her own hands, and the fire would be a beacon of protest to others. Or she could tear her bedsheets into strips and fashion a rope to hang herself. Or she could go to Nick one last time, if he would let her in.

Her predecessor is very much with her, and she feels she is not alone.

Then she hears the sound of a van approaching the house and realizes it is too late to do anything. Too late to start a fire or make a rope. There were so many things she could have done—stolen Serena Joy's knitting needles or gardening shears, a variety of weapons—but she has missed all her chances.

Nick pushes her door open, to her surprise. He tells her it's Mayday that has come, and she sees two men in the hall behind him. She can't believe it, but Nick says, "Trust me." Somehow those two words reach her. She will trust him. Besides, has she any choice?

She goes downstairs with the three men. Stunned, Serena Joy

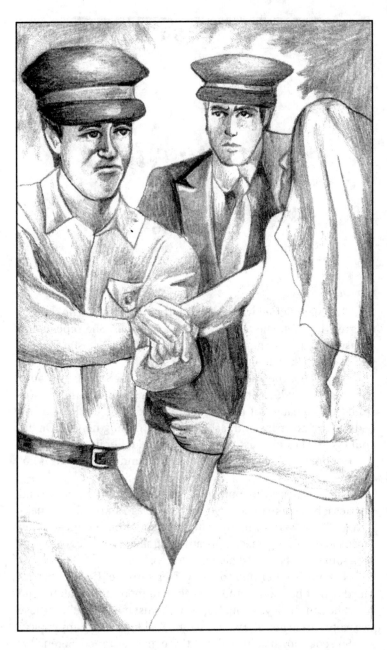

and the Commander hover in the front hall, and Offred can't help but feel pity for the Commander, who looks a wreck.

The two Eyes make an arrest, showing the Commander their authorization. Then Offred is taken out to the van and driven away.

Analysis

Offred's condemnation of herself for not taking things into her own hands—exerting control over her own destiny—raises questions about how to survive in Gilead. On the one hand, things have not gone well for those who were activists. Her mother is dead in the Colonies; Moira is doomed at Jezebel's; Ofglen has killed herself. That's where their activism has taken them. But Janine, the obedient one, obviously will die, too.

Perhaps Offred's idea of starting a fire is a valid alternative. She thinks that she will die anyway, why not burn herself in protest? Why not determine when and where her life will end?

The story's ending is ambiguous. Neither Offred nor the reader can be sure that Nick is a good guy and that the two Eyes really are members of Mayday who have come to save her. Perhaps he has been a spy all along, sent to investigate the Commander.

The Commander has broken many rules. Aside from what goes on at his home, he has taken a Handmaid—two of them, at least—to Jezebel's and flaunted her. There are resident prostitutes like Moira at Jezebel's for the hierarchy, but he brought Offred. Perhaps his colleagues are out to get him, strip him of his authority and maybe his life.

Totalitarian regimes are hothouses of intrigue, plots, and corruption. In Nazi Germany, Hitler's henchmen intrigued against each other. Himmler, head of the SS, spied on Goering. Canaris, head of intelligence, spied on Himmler and others. Hitler's secretary, Borman, spied on everyone.

Stalin is alleged to have been murdered by his security chief, Beria, as part of a plot to replace him. Then Beria was shot by his fellow conspirators.

A free society has its share of plotting and corruption, too, but it also has a free press to expose such things, and a court system to curb abuses and put the worst abusers in prison. Its voters are able to change the government at each election if they choose.

Perhaps Nick is a spy and Offred is doomed. But he may be exactly what he says he is, Offred's savior, in which case she soon will find herself alive and free, with a chance of reuniting with her family.

Her story ends with this ambiguity: is she safe or is she doomed? That Atwood chose not to end the novel here is puzzling to many readers. To them, the final chapter, "Historical Notes," is a confusing anticlimax.

Something worth noting: the only humane organizations in Gilead, Mayday and Underground Femaleroad, combined women and men working for a common goal. Atwood seems to be telling the reader: only cooperation works. It echoes John Donne's famous funeral sermon, "No man is an island." No man, and no woman either, not if he or she wants to survive.

Historical Notes

Summary

This chapter purports to be the transcript of the Twelfth Symposium on Gileadean Studies, held in 2195 at the University of Denay, Nunavit, in Canada's Northwest Territories (the Denay are a major tribe of the North). Professor Maryann Crescent Moon chairs this symposium. The main speaker is Professor James Darcy Pieixoto of Cambridge University.

Crescent Moon opens with an announcement of the other activities available later in the day, including speeches and other symposia, whose leaders almost all have non-European names. Then she introduces Pieixoto, mentioning his article, "Iran and Gilead: Two Late-Twentieth-Century Monotheocracies, as Seen through Diaries." His talk today is "Problems of Authentication in Reference to *The Handmaid's Tale*."

Pieixoto starts off with a nasty crack about Crescent Moon and lards his talk with jokes about women—for example, referring to the Underground Femaleroad as "the Underground Frailroad." He is the perfect example of a male chauvinist.

He tells his audience that Offred's book was found in an old U.S. Army-issue footlocker in Bangor, Maine. The locker held 30 tape cassettes, including "Mantovani's Mellow Strings" and "Elvis Presley's Golden Years." The first couple of tracks on each cassette is such music. But then Offred's voice cuts in and she tells her tale. Clearly Offred spent a considerable time hiding somewhere near Bangor to have taped all this. Pieixoto says that Offred's trail ends in Maine; there is no record of what happened to her after that.

He talks about the problems that overwhelmed Gilead and led to its end, but with little detail. Readers do not learn exactly when and how Gilead fell—whether it lost its various wars or was toppled by a revolution.

Pieixoto explains why Gilead came into being, and seems sympathetic to the aims of its founders: to prevent the gradual extinction of white America. He puts Offred into the context of historical change, rather than seeing her as an individual who was victimized by a fanatical regime.

He concentrates more on the Commander's identity and offers two possibilities: Frederick R. Waterford, who designed the Handmaid costume, and B. Frederick Judd, who organized the massacre of Congress and came up with the idea for Particicution.

His main message is that historians should not pass moral judgment on Gilead: it did what seemed right at the time. His philosophy seems to be, "To understand all is to forgive all," for he clearly does not condemn Gilead and feels no pity for Offred or any of Gilead's other victims.

When his speech ends, the audience of historians applaud. The novel ends with his "Are there any questions?"

Analysis

The fact that almost every name mentioned at the symposium seems Native American suggests that the world's Caucasian population has declined, perhaps close to extinction. For all its fury, Gilead failed to stop this.

But it is the unbearably smug Pieixoto who dominates this chapter, showing that sexism is alive and well in the Twenty-second Century. And nobody objects, nobody walks out on him.

Even worse is his insistence that historians be nonjudgmental about the Gilead regime. He is a moral relativist—that is, he believes there is no overriding morality, and events, institutions, and people should be seen as products of historical situations that merely reacted to events.

While there is some validity to this philosophy, clearly it's dangerous to stretch it too far. Morality does count. Otherwise one can argue that Hitler's problems with his stern, elderly father and his doting mother made him what he was, making his terrorism in

Europe an understandable acting-out of these problems—under-standable, and, therefore, forgivable. Moral relativity can excuse Stalin's, Mao's, Idi Amin's, Pol Pot's, and even Jack the Ripper's crimes.

Pieixoto ends with, "Are there any questions?" Atwood obviously wants the reader to raise questions, starting with, "Who is this creep? And why doesn't anybody object to his drivel?"

Atwood is also addressing the reader in this final sentence. Having experienced Offred's realities in Gilead through the reading, the reader is now being challenged to question and problematize misogynistic structures and attitudes in his or her own society. It is only through inquiry and challenge—as opposed to complacency—that society will rid itself of the sexist ideology that hinders both men and women from living free and fully realized lives.

Perhaps the biggest question is: Why did Atwood add this chapter, when Chapter 46 is a very fitting end? Possibly she felt readers might close the book thinking that although Gilead was an awful place, where horrible things were done, it was an isolated episode in history; and surely, people would learn from it and not allow such a horror to arise again.

So Atwood counters with a room of eminent historians, shapers of society's thoughts, who have learned absolutely nothing from Gilead's history. They look at Gilead as if they were looking through a microscope at a cancer cell—interesting, but without any moral relevance.

The American philosopher George Santayana once said, "Those who cannot remember the past are condemned to repeat it." But this audience *does* know history. It reads it and writes it, yet it is prepared to ignore history's lessons, just as the world did when it allowed ethnic murder and war to break out in Bosnia.

Perhaps these historians should read something else of Santayana's, from one of his poems:

> It is not wisdom to be only wise,
> And on the inward vision close the eyes,
> But it is wisdom to believe the heart.

Pieixoto has no heart when it comes to Offred and Gilead's other victims. Atwood seems to say that this is his crime and the crime of his audience. Only if they, and humanity in general, have a heart, can they learn from the crimes of the past and prevent the crimes of the future. Only then will there be a balm in Gilead.

Study Questions

1. Why does Offred offer two different versions of her encounter with Nick?

2. Why does Offred say that she did not behave well when speaking of her relationship with Nick?

3. Why are the Salvagings and Particicutions public ceremonies?

4. Why do the Handmaids act so murderously?

5. Why doesn't Offred take part in the Particicution?

6. What are possible reasons for Ofglen's near-arrest?

7. How does Serena Joy find out that Offred and her husband have been meeting secretly at night?

8. Who has summoned the Eyes to arrest Offred?

9. One of the events Crescent Moon announces is a nature walk. Given that the symposium takes place close to the Arctic Circle, what does this suggest?

10. What is the significance of Pieixoto's article on Iran and Gilead?

Answers

1. In one version, she and Nick immediately make passionate love; in the other, there is awkwardness and tension between them before they begin. The reader is not certain which version is accurate. Offred herself says, "All I can hope for is a reconstruction." It is possible that Offred's guilt over her betrayal of Luke keeps her from squarely facing the truth of that encounter.

2. Offred seems to be ashamed that she became so engrossed in her relationship with Nick that she became careless and complacent. She divulged secrets to Nick without being cer-

tain he was trustworthy, thereby putting people like Ofglen at potential risk.

3. Ceremony is important in people's lives, from Santa Claus parades and Fourth of July celebrations to Thanksgiving dinners. It helps give people a sense of community, a sense of what their society is all about. Gilead is about fear and blood, and its ceremonies demonstrate this. It is Gilead's way of saying, "We are all in this together, and look what happens to those who try to break loose."

4. As we have seen with Offred, everyone in Gilead feels isolated and oppressed and murderous or suicidal. This communal killing lets them act out their murderous impulses and serves as a catharsis. The victims are scapegoats upon whom the Handmaids, the most repressed people in Gilead, can act out their rage.

5. Offred doesn't participate because the thinks it is wrong. The other Handmaids have either internalized their oppression or are frightened of being picked out as rebels. They want to appear true believers. That Offred resists this response suggests that she still rejects the inhumanity of the regime, despite the complacency she demonstrated in the previous chapter.

6. It is possible that Ofglen fell under suspicion because of her unusual aggressiveness in the Particicution. Also, she may have been overheard explaining to Offred that she kicked the Guardian in the head so as to spare him the suffering of the fatal beating he was about to face. Nick could also have reported on Ofglen since Offred told him everything about her. Finally, there may have been informers in Mayday who turned her in.

7. Serena Joy finds lipstick on the cloak that her husband took from her closet for Offred to wear to Jezebel's. This must have prompted her to investigate her husband's study in which she found the sequinned outfit. This evidence leads her to conclude that once again her husband has been consorting with the Handmaid.

8. The ending is ambiguous so the reader cannot be certain of who summoned the Eyes to arrest Offred. It wasn't Serena Joy or the Commander; both are shocked to see the Eyes at their door. Nick claims that he summoned them and that they are actually people from Mayday in disguise. Nick would have had the chance to make these arrangements between the time that Serena Joy confronts Offred about her misbehavior and the time that the black van arrives. The question remains whether this is really a rescue attempt, as Nick claims, or whether he has turned her over to the authorities.

9. One of Atwood's underlying messages in the novel is that the consequences of worldwide pollution will have an impact on human health and reproduction, which, in turn, may affect the kind of government we have. Under Mao, China experienced a population explosion that led to a policy of one child per family. This was enforced by government ordered abortions and sterilization, the idea being that harsh problems required harsh solutions. America's problem, in Atwood's novel, is harsh, resulting in a government that undertook harsh and murderous solutions. Atwood likely is saying that we had better solve the environmental problem in a reasonable, democratic way while we can, or we might end up with a Gilead-like regime that will solve it the hard way. The territory where the symposium is set has a harsh climate with a very short summer. While a variety of flowers burst into bloom during that short summer, it's hardly the place for a nature walk—unless global warming, another by-product of pollution, has warmed Nunavit appreciably, giving it a climate similar to that of, say, Washington. In that case, what has Washington's climate become?

10. Pieixoto's linking Iran and Gilead, two "monotheocracies" (i.e., states with one official religion and ruled by that religion's leaders) is a clear indication of what inspired Atwood to write this novel. If such a restrictive regime could happen to Iran, an oil-rich, industrializing country with a history of secular government that looked to the West for its model, perhaps such a regime could come to power here, too. The lesson is, don't be smug and think you're immune,

as in Sinclair Lewis's *It Can't Happen Here* (1935). Lewis's novel predicted with remarkable accuracy the rise to power of an American politician identical to Senator Joseph McCarthy, whose communist-hunts terrorized many Americans in the 1950s. Will Atwood prove to be just as accurate?

Suggested Essay Topics

1. Discuss the various ways Gilead turns its people's anger and frustration away from the regime and onto some safe target—a scapegoat. Discuss other instances of such scapegoating in real life.

2. Draw a composite picture of all the opposition movements against Gilead, with their strengths and their weaknesses.

3. Compare the society of the year 2195 to the society of Gilead. In what ways have the society's values changed? In what ways have they remained the same? What is Atwood's intention in depicting this futuristic society as she does?

4. The Historical Notes strongly suggest that Offred was rescued by Mayday when she was taken from the Commander's house. What impact do the Historical Notes have upon Offred's narrative? Do they take away the ambiguity of the ending, or can the significance of these Notes be problematized? Consider Atwood's intentions in including the Historical Notes.

Sample Analytical Paper Topics

Topic #1

Many democratic governments have been overthrown in the Twentieth Century. *The Handmaid's Tale* shows how the government of the United States might be overthrown by a fanatical group and a dictatorship established. Consider how a government such as Gilead is created and how those in power attempt to maintain their control.

Outline

I. Thesis Statement: The Handmaid's Tale *illustrates that a dictatorship can be established by playing upon people's fears and dissatisfaction with societal conditions and that, once dictatorial controls are instituted, fear tactics can be asserted to attempt to keep the government in place.*

II. Dissatisfactory conditions of the pre-Gilead society

    A. Environmental deterioration due to increased pollution and nuclear explosions

    B. Increased objectification of women through pornography

    C. Increased sexual violence against women

    D. Decreased birth rate among the Caucasian population

    E. Rampant new strain of syphilis

III. Measures taken to seize control of the government and the society

    A. Use of media to promote dissatisfaction

    B. Assassination of the President and Congress

    C. Mass firing of all women and seizure of their assets

    D. Savage repression of protests

IV. Fear tactics used to maintain control in Gilead

    A. Regimentation of society

        1. Women assigned to groupings according to their function

        2. Society in uniforms, based upon groupings

        3. Elimination of choice in daily life

        4. Rivalries and jealousies between different groupings encouraged

    B. Indoctrination

        1. The Red Center

        2. Misinformation on television, the only remaining information medium

        3. Enforced illiteracy

        4. Society involved in the punishment of offenders (Salvagings)

    C. Creation of paranoia and fear

        1. Meetings, even most conversations, banned

        2. Threat of banishment to the Colonies

        3. Public display of execution victims

        4. The Eyes/the black vans

V. Resistance to government of Gilead, despite the repressive controls

    A. War in Latin America and in various states

    B. The Mayday resistance

    C. The Underground Female road

VI. Conclusion

    A. The manipulation of societal fear in establishing and maintaining a dictatorship

    B. The inevitable vulnerability of a dictatorship due to the ability of resistance movements to move beyond fear

Topic #2

Sexism and misogyny exist when women are not granted the same rights as men, when women are restricted to the domestic sphere, and when women are valued primarily for their functionality rather than their humanness. Consider the way that sexism and misogyny share the culture of Gilead as well as the societies that precede and follow it.

Outline

I. Thesis Statement: The Handmaid's Tale *presents an extreme example of sexism and misogyny by featuring the complete objectification of women in the society of Gilead. Yet by also highlighting the mistreatment of women in the cultures that precede and follow the Gileadean era, Margaret Atwood is suggesting that sexism and misogyny are deeply embedded in any society and that serious and deliberate attention must be given to these forms of discrimination in order to eliminate them.*

II. Discrimination of women in pre-Gilead society

    A. Increased objectification of women's bodies through pornography

    B. Increased sexual violence against women

    C. Growing sentiment that women are at fault for falling birth rates and for sexual violence committed against them

III. Extreme forms of misogyny in Gilead

    A. Women denied basic human rights

        1. The right to claim ownership of children

      2.   The right to work outside the home

      3.   The right to make choices in daily life (dress, friendships, sexual partners)

      4.   The right to have an abortion

      5.   The right to own property

  B. Women grouped according to their domestic functionality

      1.   Handmaids— expected to reproduce

      2.   Marthas—expected to perform household chores

      3.   Wives—expected to raise children and to enforce the rules of the domestic sphere

      4.   Econowives—lower class wives expected to carry out all three domestic functions in their homes

      5.   Women who do not have value in the domestic sphere relegated to brothels or to the Colonies

  C. The dissatisfaction of all women in Gilead

      1.   Suicide rate of the Handmaids

      2.   Bitterness of the Wives towards Handmaids and coldness towards husbands

      3.   Jealousy of the Marthas towards the Handmaids

IV. Sexism of futuristic society revealed in the Twelfth Symposium of Gileadean Studies held in 2195

  A. Speaker's joke about the Underground Frailroad and his pun on the word "tail"

  B. Speaker's interest in the possible identity of the Commander, not in the human suffering of Offred

  C. Speaker's unwillingness to pass moral judgment on Gileadeans

V. Conclusion

  A. *The Handmaid's Tale* presents an extreme form of misogyny

    B.   Echoes of this misogyny in the cultures preceding and following Gilead suggest that sexism is prevalent and deeply embedded in society

    C.   Misogyny takes a great personal toll on all people—male and female—in a sexist society

Topic #3

> *In* The Handmaid's Tale, *Margaret Atwood presents a first person narrator who chronicles her experiences under an extremely oppressive, misogynistic regime. Explore the development of this character during the course of her narrative. Does she move from fear and intimidation to the liberation of her will, or is the character formation more complicated in this text?*

Outline

I.   Thesis Statement: *Margaret Atwood's* The Handmaid's Tale *is not a narrative of a character living under repressive conditions who unambiguously moves from fear and intimidation to full-fledged resistance. Rather, Offred's character development is complex, for her desire to resist the life that has been assigned her is compromised at various points throughout this narrative. Atwood is highlighting the human impulse towards complacency in order to gain security or happiness, but she is also emphasizing the importance of resistance, regardless of the costs.*

II. Offred's resistance to activism in the days prior to the Gileadean revolution

    A.   Her desire to distance herself from her mother's feminist activism

    B.   Her complacent nature in comparison to the assertive Moira

    C.   Her naiveté about the misogynistic sentiment being fostered in the society

III. Offred's character changes during her time at the Commander's house
    A. Her initial fear and intimidation

        1. Her frequent consideration of suicide

        2. Her attachment to the previous Offred

        3. Her tenuous hold on her sanity

    B. Her growing confidence in the possibility of resistance

        1. The information about the Mayday resistance group

        2. The example provided by Ofglen

        3. Her knowledge of the Commander's weaknesses and her growing influence over him

    C. Her renewed complacency and fear of punishment

        1. Her disinterest in escape due to her attachment to Nick

        2. Her fear for herself after Serena Joy learns of her intimacies with the Commander

        3. The example of complacency provided by Moira at the club

IV. Offred's possible rescue, despite the inconsistency of her desire to resist

V.   Conclusion
    A. The difficulties of resistance, considering the human impulse towards security and happiness

    B. Atwood's emphasis—despite these difficulties—on the dangers of complacency and the need for the reader to challenge sexist structures in society

SECTION NINETEEN

Bibliography

Atwood, Margaret. *The Handmaid's Tale*. Boston: Houghton Mifflin, 1986.

REA'S
PROBLEM
SOLVERS®

The PROBLEM SOLVERS® are comprehensive supplemental textbooks designed to save time in finding solutions to problems. Each PROBLEM SOLVER® is the first of its kind ever produced in its field. It is the product of a massive effort to illustrate almost any imaginable problem in exceptional depth, detail, and clarity. Each problem is worked out in detail with a step-by-step solution, and the problems are arranged in order of complexity from elementary to advanced. Each book is fully indexed for locating problems rapidly.

Accounting	**Genetics**
Advanced Calculus	**Geometry**
Algebra & Trigonometry	**Linear Algebra**
Automatic Control Systems/Robotics	**Mechanics**
Biology	**Numerical Analysis**
Business, Accounting & Finance	**Operations Research**
Calculus	**Organic Chemistry**
Chemistry	**Physics**
Differential Equations	**Pre-Calculus**
Economics	**Probability**
Electrical Machines	**Psychology**
Electric Circuits	**Statistics**
Electromagnetics	**Technical Design Graphics**
Electronics	**Thermodynamics**
Finite & Discrete Math	**Topology**
Fluid Mechanics/Dynamics	**Transport Phenomena**

If you would like more information about any of these books, complete the coupon below and return it to us or visit your local bookstore.

REA's **Test Preps**
The Best in Test Preparation

- REA "Test Preps" are **far more** comprehensive than any other test preparation series
- Each book contains up to **eight** full-length practice tests based on the most recent exams
- **Every** type of question likely to be given on the exams is included
- Answers are accompanied by **full** and **detailed** explanations

REA publishes over 70 Test Preparation volumes in several series. They include:

**Advanced Placement
Exams (APs)**
Biology
Calculus AB & Calculus BC
Chemistry
Economics
English Language & Composition
English Literature & Composition
European History
French
Government & Politics
Physics B & C
Psychology
Spanish Language
Statistics
United States History
World History

**College-Level Examination
Program (CLEP)**
Analyzing and Interpreting
Literature
College Algebra
Freshman College Composition
General Examinations
General Examinations Review
History of the United States I
History of the United States II
Human Growth and Development
Introductory Sociology
Principles of Marketing
Spanish

SAT Subject Tests
Biology E/M
Chemistry
English Language Proficiency Test
French
German

SAT Subject Tests (cont'd)
Literature
Mathematics Level 1, 2
Physics
Spanish
United States History

Graduate Record Exams (GREs)
Biology
Chemistry
Computer Science
General
Literature in English
Mathematics
Physics
Psychology

ACT - ACT Assessment

ASVAB - Armed Services Vocational
Aptitude Battery

CBEST - California Basic Educational
Skills Test

CDL - Commercial Driver License Exam

CLAST - College Level Academic
Skills Test

COOP & HSPT - Catholic High School
Admission Tests

ELM - California State University Entry
Level Mathematics Exam

FE (EIT) - Fundamentals of Engineering
Exams - For both AM & PM Exams

FTCE - Florida Teacher Certification Exam

GED - High School Equivalency Diploma
Exam (U.S. & Canadian editions)

GMAT - Graduate Management
Admission Test

LSAT - Law School Admission Test

MAT - Miller Analogies Test

MCAT - Medical College Admission Test

MTEL - Massachusetts Tests for
Educator Licensure

NJ HSPA - New Jersey High School
Proficiency Assessment

NYSTCE: LAST & ATS-W - New York
State Teacher Certification

PLT - Principles of Learning &
Teaching Tests

PPST - Pre-Professional Skills Tests

PSAT / NMSQT

SAT

TExES - Texas Examinations of
Educator Standards

THEA - Texas Higher Education
Assessment

TOEFL - Test of English as a Foreign
Language

TOEIC - Test of English for
International Communication

USMLE Steps 1,2,3 - U.S. Medical
Licensing Exams

U.S. Postal Exams 460 & 470

Research & Education Association
61 Ethel Road W., Piscataway, NJ 08854
Phone: (732) 819-8880   **website: www.rea.com**

Please send me more information about your Test Prep books.

Name _____

Address _____

City _____ State _____ Zip _____